Best Tea ~~~p
Walks
in Cheshire

Clive Price
and Graham Beech

Second edition © Clive Price & Graham Beech 2012
First edition © Clive Price, 1995, revised 2003; with further revisons 2005

Published by Sigma Leisure – an imprint of
Sigma Press, Stobart House, Pontyclerc, Penybanc Road
Ammanford, Carmarthenshire SA18 3HP

British Library Cataloguing in Publication Data

A CIP record for this book is available from the British Library

ISBN: 978-1-85058-921-1

Typesetting and Design by: Sigma Press, Ammanford, Carms

Maps: © Bute Cartographics

Photographs: © Graham Beech, except where noted

Cover photograph: Little Moreton Hall © Graham Beech

Printed by: Berforts Group Ltd

Disclaimer: The information in this book is given in good faith and is believed to be correct at the time of publication. Care should always be taken when walking in hill country. Where appropriate, attention has been drawn to matters of safety. The author and publisher cannot take responsibility for any accidents or injury incurred whilst following these walks. Only you can judge your own fitness, competence and experience. Do not rely solely on sketch maps for navigation: we strongly recommend the use of appropriate Ordnance Survey (or equivalent) maps.

Walks

Locations of Best Teashop Walks in Cheshire

About Cheshire

In earlier editions of this book, Cheshire was a single county. In 2009, two new unitary authorities were created: "Cheshire East" and the more cumbersomely named "Cheshire West and Chester". The combined boundary, however, is much the same as before, so in this book "Cheshire" refers to the combined parts – east and west – which, together, have a blend of scenery unrivalled by few other counties. In the east are the high, bleak and windswept moorlands patterned by drystone walls and riven by deep cloughs with their tumbling streams: in the west the mudflats of the Dee estuary play host to the vast wintering populations of wading birds.

The central plain noted for its languid rivers is broken by the sandstone upthrusts of Alderley Edge and the hills of Peckforton, Bickerton, Bulkeley, Frodsham and Helsby. It is dotted with Medieval, Tudor and Jacobean architectural gems built in the celebrated black and white "Magpie" style. The green, lush pastures are grazed by countless herds of Friesians which produce the milk used in that gourmet's delight, Cheshire Cheese.

Chester with its Roman remains and medieval walls, Nantwich with brine springs and cathedral style parish church and Sandbach noted for its stone crosses, add an extra dimension to the countless villages with names redolent of rural England – Bunbury, Burwardsley, Tarporley, Malpas, Cholmondley, Audlem and Wybunbury.

Canals

The late eighteenth century saw the construction of several canals across Cheshire including the pioneering Bridgewater Canal in the north which gave birth to the era of Canal Mania. Others which followed were the Macclesfield, the Trent and Mersey and several shorter ones which were later amalgamated into the Shropshire Union with its branch to Llangollen, often referred to as the Llangollen Canal.

This is not the place to discuss the history of these but, even though commercial traffic no longer plies these waterways they are all used extensively by pleasure boats.

More importantly, they have bequeathed a legacy of tow-paths which, in recent years, have been repaired and upgraded for use by walkers. In this collection several stretches have been used to provide useful links between other paths in order that circular routes could be devised. In most cases, they pass through some delightful scenery, thereby adding an extra dimension to the walk.

The Walks

These routes enable the walker to explore the rich tapestry of the Cheshire countryside at leisure, often allowing him or her to discover hidden corners of great beauty which are denied to the motorist.

For those in search of challenge there are tough uphill routes, especially those through the moorland districts in the east of the county and those traversing the sandstone ridges. However, for the most part, they are easy walks ideally suited for parents with young children or for those preferring gentle strolls in the evenings or on hot, lazy afternoons. Few are longer than five miles thereby allowing ample time for observation of the points of historical interest and wildlife along the way. Of course, no walk would be complete without frequent pauses to admire the scenery and the views of which there is an abundance.

Important note: many stiles are being replaced by kissing gates – please be aware of this when following the directions.

The Teashops

There is no pleasanter way to end a country walk than by having a leisurely cream tea or even just a cuppa. Everybody has their ideal of what a country café should be but, as in other walks of life, even the cafés are changing. The cosy establishment with linen tablecloths and bone china may still be found but others are of the self service variety.

Cafés are not as widespread as they once were although some new ones opened their doors whilst this book was in preparation. Sadly, others closed. It is their distribution that has dictated the locations of the walks included in this selection. One is housed in a medieval monastic refectory, another reflects the age of the Penny Farthing while a third has a truly Dickensian atmosphere. In others you can enjoy your tea in the station waiting room as the trains roll by, absorb the atmosphere of an eighteenth century cotton mill or contemplate your purchase of a Royal Worcester dinner service.

No matter which you choose you can be certain of an afternoon tea with irresistible mouth-watering cakes and other delights, all home-baked and accompanied by a large pot of freshly brewed tea. Alternatively you may prefer a morning coffee or light lunch when you will also be assured of a warm, welcoming environment.

The opening times listed for each café or restaurant were correct at the time of writing and were re-checked as late as possible. However, they may change. So, before embarking on your walk it may be as well if you check with the establishment. To facilitate this the telephone numbers have been listed. Please note that some cafés open for shorter hours during the winter months while some close completely.

PLEASE, as an act of courtesy and common sense, remove your muddy boots before entering because many of the tea rooms are luxuriously carpeted.

Tourist Information

Cheshire is rich in tourist attractions ranging from the Roman remains in the City of Chester through the collection of medieval churches to such modern developments as Jodrell Bank with its radio telescope and planetarium.

References to most of these are included in the text but there is no space in a book of this type to provide details of all of these but information about all of them may be obtained from **www.cheshireeast.gov.uk** and **www.cheshirewestandchester.gov.uk**

Tourist Information Centres are located at:

Chester:
Town Hall, Northgate Street, Chester, Cheshire CH1 2HJ
enquiries@cheshirewestandchester.gov.uk. Tel: 0845 647 7868

Congleton:
Town Hall, High Street, Congleton, CW12 1BN
congletontic@cheshireeast.gov.uk; Tel: 01260 271095

Macclesfield:
Market Place, Macclesfield SK10 1DX
macclesfieldtic@cheshireeast.gov.uk. Tel: 01625 378123

Nantwich:
Civic Hall, Market Street, Nantwich CW5 5DG
Tel: 0300 123 5500

Northwich:
1 The Arcade, Northwich, Cheshire CW9 5AS
Tel: 01606 353534

Most local libraries have leaflets and details of local tourist attractions.

Public Transport

All the walks in this book are accessible by public transport and details are provided about bus or train services at the start of each route. Current information is available on Bus, Train and Coach times is available from Cheshire Traveline on 0871 200 22 33. (7 days a week 8am – 8pm; closed Christmas Day, Boxing Day and New Year's Day). Detailed information about train times may be obtained by ringing National Rail Enquiries on 08457 48 49 50 or online from **www.nationalrail.co.uk**

Clothing and Equipment

Good clothing and equipment will not only increase your safety prospects but also add to your enjoyment. Obviously clothing is mainly a matter of personal choice but there are some general guidelines. Jeans, for example, are not advisable in wet, cold weather because they can be a serious hazard in combating hypothermia.

A good pair of walking boots or shoes is essential, even on lower ground where paths can be very muddy, especially after a prolonged period of wet weather. Any good stockist will offer a wide range so you can choose to suit your pocket.

Sandles and high heeled shoes are not suitable for country walking. They offer no protection against wet conditions and increase the possibility of a twisted ankle. Remember that walking boots have specially designed treads to increase their grip in slippery conditions. It is advisable to wear two pairs of walking socks so allow for this when buying your boots.

Because the British climate is so variable a cagoule and over-trousers should be carried at all times. Again go for quality when buying but avoid cheaper varieties which may cause undue condensation. Today there is a choice of breathable fabrics such as Gore-Tex and Sympatex, but they are expensive.

An extra pullover is another essential because on the higher ground the temperature is always a few degrees lower than in the valley bottoms. Clothing should not to be too tightly fitting but reasonably loose and comfortable. Avoid anything which will catch on barbed wire or hedges.

In winter, when conditions may be far more severe, extra clothing should be worn. Two light pullovers are warmer than a single heavy one. Extremities should be covered because it is from these that the greatest loss of body-heat occurs. A warm woolly hat, which can be pulled down over the face and ears is a must. Gloves should be worn.

Always carry a first-aid kit in case of cuts or minor accidents. Another useful item is a pocket knife. On most of these walks you are unlikely to encounter problems but, to call for assistance, a whistle is a useful tool.

Again food is a matter of personal choice but ensure that at all times you carry some emergency rations in the form of chocolate bars which will provide energy in case of delay.

A good day sack should prove more than adequate for all the walks contained in this selection.

Walk 1: Parkgate

Route	Old Baths - Gayton - Backwood Hall - Brookhouse - Wirral Way - Old Quay - The Parade - Old Baths
Start	The Old Baths car park, Parkgate, Wirral. Map reference SJ274789
Distance	6½ miles
Map	OS Explorer 266, Wirral & Chester/Caer
Getting there by public transport	Parkgate has frequent daily buses from Chester, Birkenhead, Hoylake and Meols. No Sunday service
Getting there by car	Parkgate is approached by either the B5134, the B5135 or the B5136 from the A540 Chester to Hoylake road. There is a small car park off Mostyn Square in the centre of the village but the Old Baths car park, just beyond the Boat House pub, usually has spare places

The Tea Shop

The Parkgate Coffee Shop on the Parade not only offers a fine view out over the Dee Estuary but also provides everything from a cup of tea to substantial snacks. Run by Suzanne Hughes, it has a mouth-watering selection of home-made cakes and some of the best scones (served with clotted cream) you are likely to see in Cheshire. Housed in one of the old seafront houses, it comes complete with wooden beams and photos of Parkgate in bygone days. There is an autographed photograph of Sir Paul McCartney behind the counter as a souvenir of his visit to the coffee shop.

Opening Hours: Tuesday to Friday, 9.30am to 4.30pm; Saturday and Sunday, 10am to 5pm. Closed Mondays. Tel: 0151 336 4414.

Parkgate

When the River Dee silted up and large ships were no longer able to reach Chester, Parkgate became the chief port of embarkation for Ireland. At high tide it was not unknown for the Parade to be flooded. During the nineteenth century it also developed as a fashionable resort.

Mostyn House, Parkgate

Today it is no longer a port, separated from the narrow channel of the river by enormous grass and reed covered marshes which are the haunt of thousands of wading birds in winter. The front is lined with attractive houses and cottages and it is renowned for the shellfish on sale in some of the fish shops.

The large black and white house, now Mostyn House School, was once a hotel where Handel stayed while waiting for a packet boat to Dublin for the first performance of his "Messiah".

Lady Hamilton was born near Parkgate so, according to local tradition, Admiral Nelson may have sailed into Parkgate for a romantic tryst.

The Route

Leave the Old Baths car park to proceed through the picnic area in a northerly direction with the silted-up River Dee on your left. The course of the river is an apparently endless mass of grass and other vegetation. Do not be tempted to walk on this because it is full of quicksand and riven by numerous water courses.

On your right is hawthorn, ragwort and an abundance of guelder rose beyond which is a golf course. This, in turn, gives way to a succession of

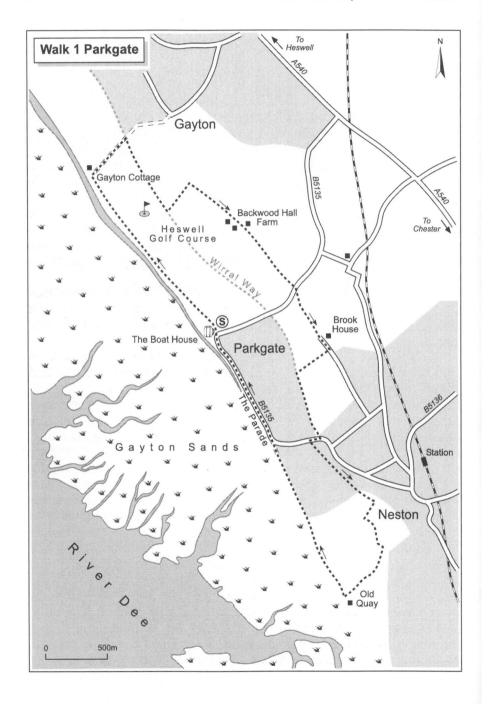

open fields. Ignore a sign on your right to the Wirral Way and, after a little over a mile and by a white house, the path curves round to the right before descending a flight of six steps onto the end of a minor road.

Walk along this away from the River Dee, passing "Gayton Cottage" on your left, and proceeding for a quarter of a mile until it climbs slightly to cross a railway bridge. About 50 metres beyond this turn right through a waymarked gap and double back to reach the bed of a former railway track. This is the Wirral Way. Turn left.

This 12-mile walking trail follows the line of the axed railway from Hooton in Cheshire to West Kirby in Merseyside. Guide books are available from Tourist Information Centres in the area.

After negotiating the gap in a wooden barrier, the Wirral Way dips into a shallow hollow and climbs again to cross a wide track linking two sections of the golf course. 100 metres beyond this intersection, and with wooden gates flanking both sides of the track, turn left through a waymarked wooden kissing gate.

Follow the path over the links, staying between the two lines of thin blue poles. Climb gradually through a line of trees and to the left of a solitary sandstone gatepost before ascending a flight of three steps on the boundary of the golf course.

At the top turn right to follow a distinct path through a belt of trees but, after 100 metres, swing to the right over a planked footbridge and then turn sharp left to proceed along the very edge of the golf course.

There is a hedge and fence on your left matched, on your right, by a fine perspective out over the Dee Estuary to the Welsh coast with the Clywydian hills forming the backdrop. The grass path makes for excellent walking.

Negotiate a waymarked ladder stile before following the obvious path over the centre of a field to reach a footbridge with a stile at either end. Climb to the left of a fence for 50 metres to a small white wooden gate. Through that continue for a further 50 metres along a wide track to a black and white wooden gate and then maintain direction to the left of the red sandstone wall which forms the boundary of Backwood Hall, the farm on your right. Remain with this track, which develops into a hedged lane, until it meets Boathouse Lane by a footpath finger post.

Cross directly into Wood Lane, remaining with it beyond the end of Brook Lane which comes in from Brook House on your left. About 100 metres beyond, turn right through waymarked wooden posts onto a fenced path. A few metres before a bridge which spans the path, veer right up another path which leads onto the Wirral Way after 10 metres.

Turn left over the bridge. Where the Wirral Way appears to reach a dead-end, turn left through a wooden barrier and then turn right to arrive at a gate after 100 metres. This provides an exit onto Station Road.

Turn right for a few metres. Pass the Parkgate village sign and the Conservation Area sign with its full-rigged sailing ship, and then make a left turn by the Wirral Country Park sign to re-join the Wirral Way.

At the top of the approach to the former Parkgate Railway Station, where the surfaced road bends sharply to the left towards the toilet block, stay forward through a wooden barrier. Initially there are tennis courts on your right before the route pursues its course between birch and other trees, passes under an arched bridge and through another wooden barrier before reaching an intersection.

Ignore the path to the left signed to Neston. Instead make a right turn to pass a fairly inconspicuous sign which reads, "To Old Quay Lane".

The well-defined path traverses open country between a fence on the left and a hedgerow on the right until it meets Old Quay Lane. Turn left along this narrow surfaced road leading to the Sewage Treatment Works owned by Welsh Water PLC. However, do not proceed as far as the plant.

Where the road bends acutely to the right, maintain your direction through an old metal kissing gate adjacent to a (currently) decrepit metal gate. Through this, and ignoring the path leading directly ahead, fork right through a hedge gap and then veer left over the open field following another well-trodden path until it forms a T-junction in mid field with a wider grass track. Turn right along this, cross a footbridge and continue across the next field to the right of a hedge before negotiating a second metal kissing gate.

Beyond, maintain direction until reaching a small flight of stone steps. There, turn right along the path which charts a course through the substantial stone remnants of the old quay.

Add a little romance to your excursion by pausing a while to imagine sailing ships from all four corners of the globe once berthing at this point to discharge and load their cargoes. Then it would have been a bustling, thriving spot livened by the creaking of ships' timbers and the rumble of cart wheels. Today it is a scene of peace and tranquillity. The remains are surrounded by green fields and, where the river once flowed there is a sea of reeds and grass where the flocks of goldfinch and other birds roost.

Through the ruins follow the path across an area of scrub. Over the first stile, keep to the narrow path which clings close to the fence until, after half a mile and facing a bungalow, it swings round to the right to emerge into a modern housing estate by Old Quay Close.

Turn left along Manorial Road, ignoring the fact that it is signed as a cul-de-sac. At the far end continue along the path signed, "To The Parade". After 100 metres this widens into an unadopted road.

By a large black and white house turn right to a T-junction. Turn left along Hunter's Close and, with the cricket ground on your right, advance to re-join Station Road opposite a row of old fishermen's cottages. Turn left for 100 metres before turning right along the Parade.

This is the time to treat yourself to a cream tea in the Parkgate Coffee Shop, to admire the architecture, to sample the seafood in the fish shops and to absorb the view.

At the far end, where the road bends to the right, stay forward and, keeping the Boat House pub on your left, walk the final 200 metres to your starting point.

Walk 2: Willaston

Route	Hadlow Lane car park - Willaston Grange - Chester High Road - Foxes Farm - Hallwood Farm - Oak Farm - Hadlow Lane
Start	Wirral Way car park, Hadlow Lane, Willaston, Wirral. Map reference SJ331773
Distance	4½ miles
Map	OS Explorer 266, Wirral & Chester/Caer
Getting there by public transport	Willaston village is less than a quarter of a mile from the starting point. It is served by daily buses from Chester, Parkgate, West Kirby, Meols and Heswall. There are daily buses (not Sundays) from Ellesmere Port. Some buses connect at Hooton with trains from Chester, Birkenhead and Liverpool
Getting there by car	The start is off Hadlow Lane, Willaston, from where it is signed as Wirral Country Park. Both the village and car park are signed from the A540 at map reference SJ326763. The Country Park is also signed from the centre of Willaston village which stands on the B5133

The Tea Shop

Aston's café is on the main street, just a short stroll from Hadlow Lane car park. Run by Vicky Patto, it has a modern interior and some seating in the garden for summer days. There's a breakfast snack selection for early risers, baguettes and jacket potatoes at lunchtime and a specials board displays the day's freshly-made main meals. For mid-morning and afternoon tea, there are scones and a selection of tempting cakes.

Opening Hours: Monday to Thursday 9am to 4.30pm , Friday 9am to 4pm and Saturday 9 to 2pm. Closed on Sundays, so it's useful to know that the walk passes Gordale Garden Centre, which has a café that's open every day.

Willaston

Willaston is an attractive village in the middle of the Wirral Peninsula with a half timbered inn dating from the reign of Charles I and small cottages clustered around a green. Willaston Hall is even older and is renowned for its splendid Elizabethan front. The church which is built in the Gothic style dates from the nineteenth century and is distinguished by its very steep roof and its bellcot.

The Route

After having had a look around the restored station of Hadlow Road, complete with its 1950s atmosphere, proceed to the far end of the car park, pass through the barrier and continue for approximately 50 metres to a wooden finger post.

The signal box at Hadlow Road

The single arm indicates a path to Wallcroft which heads off to the left. Ignore this, choosing rather to make a right turn across the horse riders' track to negotiate a facing stile before traversing the first field while keeping close to a large barn and silo tower on your right.

Over the next stile, cross a lane to a facing waymarked stile and continue in the same direction to the left of a fence and hedge. On the far side of this field cross the planked footbridge to a footpath sign and stile which provides an exit onto New Hey Lane, a minor road.

Turn right for about 150 metres to another footpath sign. By this make a left turn over a footbridge, negotiate a waymarked stile and proceed along the boundary of a field passing Willaston Grange with its tennis courts to your right.

Beyond the next stile maintain direction over a cultivated field and remain to the left of a cottage before arriving at a rough track. Cross this directly to a very low waymarker post and continue through a belt of trees while remaining to the immediate left of a high brick wall.

On meeting another track, after 100 metres cross to a waymarked wooden stile before continuing along the right-hand side of a long, narrow

paddock where horses graze. Beyond the next stile, stay forward over another cultivated field whilst aiming for a hedge corner where, eventually, you will find a stile. Over this, turn left through ninety degrees and, staying close to the hedge on your right and circling round a large pond, continue until another stile permits an exit onto the A540, known at this point as "The Chester High Road".

Turn left and, walking along the pavement, reach the Gordale Garden Centre – particularly useful on a Sunday when the café at the start is closed. Continue along the A540, passing Burton Nurseries – another possible refreshment stop. Some 10 metres before a sign indicating a side road to Ness Gardens and Burton look for a footpath finger post on your left. By this, turn left through a metal kissing gate and, clinging to the field boundary, advance along the whole length of the field, keeping a wary eye open for the bull which, according to the notice, is present in the field.

Over the stile in the far corner stay to the left of a hedge but, over the next stile, veer right towards an obvious gateway with a large circular galvanised metal cattle trough some three metres to its left. Proceed through the gate to enter a lane which leads beyond Foxes Farm and an equestrian tack shop before passing to the left of Hallwood Farm to meet a minor road on a right-angled bend.

Do not go quite as far as the road. Instead, turn left along the driveway to Oak Farm which, according to the notices, has a fine herd of Friesian cattle. After almost half a mile along this surfaced lane keep to the left of Oak Farm and maintain direction through the farm yard. After a second metal gate the track becomes an ordinary country lane.

Pass to the right of a third gate, where a smaller one for pedestrian access is missing. Keep forward for a further 20 metres to another minor road, also on a sharp bend. Turn left along this road which, just beyond "July Cottage", provides the only climb of the walk as it rises for 100 metres to pass over a redbrick bridge spanning a disused railway line.

A hundred metres beyond the bridge, and at the bottom of the slope and by a footpath sign, make an acute turn to the left. Pass through the wooden barrier after 100 metres and turn right along the Wirral Way. Now well-established, this popular walking route is acquiring a mature vegetation which includes several varieties of tree and such plants as guelder rose, giant hogweed, bramble and rosebay willowherb.

In spring and early summer the trees resound to the calls of wrens, blackbirds, thrushes, titmice and the ubiquitous magpie with its cousin, the jay. Follow the track, eschewing any side paths, until reaching your starting point at Hadlow Road station.

Walk 3: Chester

Route	Northgate car park - Upper Northgate - City Walls - Newgate - Souter's Lane - The Groves - Old Dee Bridge - Bridge Street - The Cross - Eastgate - St Werburgh Street - Abbey Gate - Northgate - Northgate car park
Start	Northgate long stay car park, off Northgate Avenue. Map reference SJ403671
Distance	3½ miles
Map	OS Explorer 266, Wirral & Chester/Caer Town street plan from the Tourist Information Centre
Getting there by public transport	Chester is served by daily buses from London, Manchester, Liverpool, Birkenhead, Nantwich, Shrewsbury, Whitchurch, Northwich, Wrexham and Stoke-on-Trent and other towns as well as numerous local services. The bus station is off Northgate, close to the starting point of the walk. There are trains from London, Manchester, Liverpool, North Wales, Shrewsbury, Whitchurch, Liverpool, Birkenhead, Northwich and Crewe
Getting there by car	Chester is at the focal point of several major roads including the M53/56 from Birkenhead and Manchester, the A41 from the Wirral and Whitchurch, the A5104 from Mold, the A483 from Wrexham, the A61 from Nantwich, the A54 from Middlewich and Congleton and the A556 from Manchester. Apart from the Northgate long stay car park there are several others in and around the city but some are short stay only

The Tea Shop

There are several excellent tea shops and cafés in the city area but the most unusual is the Refectory café (to which there is no entrance charge). Reached through the Cathedral and the Cloisters this spacious and atmospheric tea room is housed in the thirteenth century Refectory, the dining room used by the monks of this Benedictine Abbey before Henry VIII's Reformation led to it being converted into the present Cathedral of St Werburgh to serve the newly created Diocese of Chester. It must be the only tea shop in Britain that boasts a genuine pulpit. From this one of the monks would read passages from the Bible while his brethren ate their meals in silence.

A huge tapestry on the west wall shows St Paul confronting the sorcerer Elymas on Cyprus. Woven at Mortlake during the seventeenth century it is based on a drawing by Raphael. The arms of the powerful Earls of Chester are featured in a heraldic display on the north wall.

In sharp contrast to the frugal fare of the medieval diners the Refectory today offers a menu that is positively sinful. Morning cofee is accompanied by light snacks, while lunches include items such as steak and mushroom pie and lasagne, not to mention the daily specials.

For the afternoon walker, delicacies include scones with an abundance of cream, cakes and a choice of speciality teas. Any medieval monastic ghosts hovering about the place must assume that every day is Christmas.

Opening hours: 1st April to 31st October, 9.30am to 4.30p.m; Sundays 12noon to 4pm. Tel: 01244 500979

Chester

It can truly be said that the history of Chester is the history of England in miniature. Roman garrison, site of a powerful medieval abbey transformed into a cathedral at the Reformation, bustling port during the Middle Ages that provided the gateway to Ireland, Marcher town fortified against the marauding Welsh, site of the last major conflict of the Civil War, an important coaching and later railway centre and county town, Chester has always been a vibrant, thriving city.

Today the visitor may enjoy the legacy of this rich tapestry which history has bequeathed to Chester. The Roman ruins, the Cathedral, the plethora of splendid black and white Tudor buildings, the riverside and the Rows – Europe's first undercover shopping mall – all combine to give the city a unique charm.

The Route

From the car park entrance turn left along Northgate Avenue and, at the first junction, turn left again into Victoria Avenue to pass Abbey Gate School on your right.

Keeping the Northgate Arena on your left, follow the pavement round to the left until reaching a pedestrian subway. Descend the steps, turn

Walk 3 Chester

N

Northgate
Arena

A5268

St Oswald's Way

A56

A5268

Shropshire Union Canal

Northgate Street

City Walls

St Martin's Way

Cinema

Cathedral

Town Hall Square

Town
Hall

Foregate St

The
Cross

Eastgate St

Chester
Grosvenor
Hotel

Watergate Street

Nicholas Street

Bridge Street

A5268

Lower Bridge Street

Soutter's Lane

River Dee

FB

Museum

Crown
Court

County
Hall

The Castle

Old Dee
Bridge

A483

0　　　　　200m

right at the bottom and, at the far end of the tunnel, turn right up another flight of steps. On emerging at street level stay forward to a large traffic island with fountains in the centre.

Here turn left into Upper Northgate Street soon passing the Bluecoat School on your right and crossing over the Shropshire Union Canal by a high bridge. A short distance to your right is the narrow Bridge of Sighs once used by condemned felons on their way to the Chapel of Little St John shortly before execution.

Immediately afterwards go under the sandstone arch of Northgate and turn sharp left up the steps. At the top make a right turn to follow the City Walls which, although repaired and rebuilt several times, have protected Chester since Roman times.

The shops on your right soon give way to Abbey Green followed by the Dean's Garden and a cricket field. The sound of leather on willow has replaced the clash of steel created by soldiers in training because the garrison's barracks occupied this site two thousand years ago. In summer pleasure craft ply the canal which is a long way down below on your left. Despite its proximity to the city centre it is also graced by mallard, coot and moorhen.

By the first corner stands King Charles' Tower, a reconstructed medieval building, now housing a souvenir shop and museum but from which Charles I watched his troops being defeated at the Battle of Rowton Moor in 1645. From the tower continue along the walls but now in a southerly direction with the Cathedral a short distance to the right. Climb the short flight of steps leading up to the celebrated Clock Tower which spans Eastgate. Built in 1897 to commemorate Queen Victoria's Diamond Jubilee, this affords a bird's eye view along Eastgate with its collection of black and white buildings, many dating to Tudor and even medieval times.

Continue along the walls to Newgate which crosses over St John Street with the Roman Amphitheatre down below on your left. Cross the bridge before descending the steps into Park Street. At the bottom turn right into Little St John Street and, after 10 metres, make another right turn for a visit to the Roman Gardens with their collection of imperial stone columns and hypercaust.

Leave the gardens by the same entrance and make a right turn along Little St John Street. After ten metres turn right into Souter's Lane which is signed to the River Dee and provides a passageway to The Groves.

By the landing stage used by the pleasure cruisers, turn left along the Groves with its large collection of seats and bandstand.

On approaching the conspicuous white metal suspension bridge, veer left a few metres before it to make a sharp turn to the right onto the bridge itself.

This footbridge, one of the famous landmarks of the Chester waterfront, was built in 1923 to link the city with the suburb of Handbridge.

At the far end turn right, descend a flight of steps and turn left along the riverside path. With the Dee graced by its swans on your right, pass the restored mill water wheel and an enormous weir to reach the Old Dee Bridge.

This occupies the site of a Roman bridge and was worthy of a mention in that national inventory, the Domesday Book, in 1086. The original structure, presumably of wood, was replaced by stone in 1387 and for hundreds of years remained the only bridge spanning the Dee at Chester. It was widened by the Victorians but retained its medieval appearance and today's single line traffic is regulated by lights.

Climb the short flight of steps opposite the Roman shrine to

East Street Clock

Minerva to exit onto Handbridge. Turn right over the Old Dee Bridge and keeping the Castle, now rebuilt as an assize court on your left, maintain your direction into Lower Bridge Street.

Whilst climbing this historic street you will pass "The Bear and Billet", built in 1664, "Ye Olde King's Head" from 1662 and Gamul House where a brick facade conceals a Jacobean Hall. This was the home of Sir Francis Gamul who was Mayor of Chester in 1635 and it was here, in September, 1645, that Charles I lodged on the eve of the Battle of Rowton Moor.

Further along you will also pass the early eighteenth-century Oddfellows Hall and the Toy Museum which houses a collection of Victorian dolls, teddy bears and 1920s pedal cars alongside train sets and Dinky cars. It is a veritable Aladdin's Cave for young children and those adults possessed of a strong sense of nostalgia.

At the junction of Bridge Street with Grosvenor Street and Pepper Street stands the Chester Heritage Centre housed in the former St Michael's Church. It relates the story of the city over the last 2,000 years through displays and audio-visual presentations.

Immediately on your left, and on the opposite corner to the Heritage Centre, is "The Falcon", a half-timbered seventeenth century building formerly used as a Temperance Room. Restored and ironically converted into a pub in 1982, it has won one of the highest conservation accolades, a Europa Nostra Award for the work carried out.

From this interesting cross roads continue forwards into Bridge Street, passing even more examples of black and white magpie architecture and meeting the first of the celebrated Rows.

Furious debates still persist over the reasons behind these covered shopping arcades but the stone undercrofts appear to have been built in the late thirteenth century, shortly after the Great Fire of 1278 which destroyed most of the city.

Stay with Bridge Street as far as The Cross. This, the traditional centre of Chester, stands at the junction of the four main streets, Eastgate, Northgate, Bridge Street and Watergate. As its name implies, Watergate led down to the harbour in the years when Chester was a thriving port.

The Cross was carved from local sandstone in the fifteenth century and has been restored following damage during the Civil War. It is now used as the principal station for the Town Crier at midday and at three o'clock every afternoon from Tuesday to Saturday between Easter and the end of September. By The Cross turn right along Eastgate and then turn left into the very narrow Godstall Lane, staying with it until emerging into St Werburgh Street opposite the Cathedral entrance.

Turn left along St Werburgh Street following it round until it forms a junction with Northgate opposite the imposing Town Hall. Turn right to retrace your steps to the starting point.

Walk 4: Frodsham

Route	Beacon Hill - Shepherd's cottage - Dober's Lane - Riley Bank - Snidley Moor - Woodhouse Hill - Dunsdale Hollow - Jacob's Ladder - Beacon Hill
Start	Beacon Hill car park, Frodsham. Map reference SJ518766
Distance	4 miles
Map	OS Explorer 267, Northwich & Delamere Forest
Getting there by public transport	Frodsham is served by frequent daily (including Sundays) buses from Chester, Runcorn, Widnes, and Warrington. Buses from Northwich Mondays to Saturdays. Frodsham has frequent daily (including Sundays) trains from Chester, Manchester Piccadilly, Liverpool, Warrington and Runcorn
Getting there by car	Frodsham is located on the A56, Chester to Warrington road. It is also signed from Junction 12 of the M56 Motorway. There are several car parks in the town centre, in addition to the starting point at Beacon Hill. Parking may be difficult on Thursday, which is market day

The Tea Shops

Though there are no tea shops on the walk, there is a choice in Frodsham itself.

The Cottage Tea Shop, standing on the north side of Main Street, lives up to its name. The owners have created a warm atmosphere: tables with spindle-backed chairs, a genuine beamed ceiling typical of the building's antiquity, and small decorated wall niches.

There is a wide range of speciality teas, brewed in large pots, and a selection of coffees and other beverages. Light meals and snacks are available while you can choose between an afternoon tea and a Cream Tea with a variety of home-made cakes rarely found elsewhere. These include carrot cake, chocolate cake, Victoria sponge and a lemon meringue pie that dissolves in the mouth.

Opening hours: All year. Mondays to Saturday, 9.30am to 4.00pm; Closed on Sundays; Tel: 01928 733673

Coffee & Cakes is in Eddisbury Square, a shopping precinct just 200 metres up Church Street leading up from the south side of Main Steet. This modern café offers a wide range of dishes including a traditional breakfast menu, lunch with home-made soup, salads, freshly made sandwiches and jacket potatoes and plenty of choice at morning coffee or afternoon tea with pastries, home-made cakes and a wide range of teas and coffees. (if you like the cakes, it's worth noting that the shop supplies superb "celebration cakes" for weddings, birthdays and other special occasions.

The Cottage Tea Shop

Opening hours: Monday to Friday, 9.00am to 5.00pm; Saturday, 9.30 am to 4.00pm; Sunday 9.30am to 3.00pm. Tel: 01928 732988.

Coffee & Cakes

Frodsham

The presence of several hill forts behind the town suggests that the settlements in this area were of ancient origin. Frodsham also stands on the route of the Roman road from Chester to Wilderspool, near Warrington.

The Norman Earls of Chester constructed a fort in the town which survived until the seventeenth century. Its site is now occupied by Castle Park. Frodsham's importance during the coaching era is recalled by such inns as the "Bear's Paw", obviously the scene of bear baiting, and the Queen's Hotel (which also serves afternoon teas). The parish church is of Norman origin.

Walk 4 Frodsham

To Warrington

Cottage Cafe ■

Station

Church Street

B5439

Frodsham

M56

To Chester

Howey Lane

P Beacon Hill

S

A56

B5393

B5152

Fivecrosses

Jacob's Ladder

B5393

Mickledale Farm ■

Woodhouse Hill

Shepherd's Cottage ■

Snidley Hill

0   500m

The Route

To avoid a steep climb of more than a mile through the suburban streets of Frodsham, it is suggested that you start from Beacon Hill, the northern terminus of the Sandstone Trail. To reach it from Main Street, Frodsham, turn into Church Street, proceeding uphill before making a right turn into Church Road, which is signed to the parish church.

Opposite the church turn left into Bellemonte Road and follow this around its tortuous course until reaching Beacon Hill car park located immediately beneath the massive radio towers.

From Beacon Hill car park make a left turn along Simoons Lane, soon passing Overhill Cottage on your left. Ignore a three-armed finger post, continuing until approximately 50 metres beyond the entrance to Frodsham Golf Club on your right.

By the footpath sign go right over the stile to keep close company with the boundary fence of the golf club which is on the right. Beyond the next stile the path continues between a hedge and a fence as it climbs gradually to provide a view of the Welsh Hills in the far distance ahead.

Ignore a stile and signed path running off to the left, staying forward to rendezvous with the lane which leads to Mickledale Farm. Cross to the facing stile before veering gradually left with the distinct path as it crosses a field to a stile by a footpath sign.

This provides an exit onto Manley Road. Turn right for 100 metres but, by Shepherd's Houses, turn left into Dober's Lane, a sandy track. Climb gradually to the left of Harrol Edge with its underground reservoir until meeting a minor road on a sharp bend.

Ignore this road. Instead turn sharp right into an unsigned lane which runs just below the reservoir. Eventually it loses height to another minor road. Turn right for a short climb to a Y-junction.

Fork right for the descent of Riley's Bank, with Riley Bank Mews on your left, to reach the B5393. Cross the T-junction to a facing ladder stile and descend the field gradually while staying close to the fence on your right. Towards the far end of this field the path suddenly corkscrews steeply down a bank to a ladder stile in a hollow.

Over the stile remain with the distinct path, curving to the right as directed by the yellow waymarker, to lose even more height through a wooded clough until reaching two separate waymarker posts in the bottom of a valley which has an atmosphere of utter remoteness.

Turn left along the broad track running along the valley floor. Negotiate a stile adjacent to a metal gate and stay forward, the slope on your right being carpeted with bracken which creates an ideal habitat for the wrens and robins to be observed along this stretch of the route.

On reaching a Y-junction fork left, remaining on the lower ground just to the right of a wire fence and parallel with some overhead wires.

Arriving at another stile alongside a metal gate, navigate carefully. Over the stile ignore a steep track going off at right angles. Instead, advance about six metres before turning right through another gate, as indicated by a faded waymark, to walk a wide lane hedged on your left and fenced on your right.

This track runs parallel with The Ridgeway, a short distance away on the crest of the slope to your left. As the name suggests, this is an ancient route but, sadly for today's walker, it is a surfaced road.

After a mere 50 metres the track passes through a gateway. On the far side turn sharply to the left and clinging closely to the hedge, follow a narrower path along the bottom of a sloping field until a stile provides access to a lane.

Turn right along this, a part of the Sandstone Trail. It climbs gradually for more than a mile through the woodlands of Snidley Moor, large swathes of which have recently been re-planted by the owners, the Woodland Trust.

It is refreshing to see a discreet notice, informing members of the public that they are free to wander through the trees flanking both sides and, to prove that this is no empty invitation, several paths rise up the steep slopes.

The Sandstone Trail continues its meandering upwards course through the woods guided by frequent waymarks. Large blocks of red sandstone are often embedded in the surface.

On arriving at a Y-junction close to the summit of Snidley Moor, fork left for 20 metres to a T-junction. Turn left as the track continues rising, this time up the slopes of Woodhouse Hill.

A brief opening in the woodland on your right permits a view of Beacon Hill but soon the route swings round to the right and re-enters more woodland to cross the site of Woodhouse Hill Fort, constructed during the Iron Age by some of Cheshire's earliest inhabitants.

The track emerges from the woods onto the summit of a sheer, high cliff where one of the finest views in Cheshire literally takes your breath away. You gaze out over the M56 Motorway to the vast expanse of Frodsham Marshes, one of the most significant ornithological sites in Britain. Beyond, the Mersey forms an enormous sweep into its estuary as it separates Lancashire from the Wirral and approaches Liverpool with the distinctive towers of its twin cathedrals dominating the distant skyline.

Having absorbed the vista, descend steeply for 50 metres to a waymarker post and turn right and walk along the cliff edge. If you have children do not let them run freely at this point.

Soon, the path meets and runs just to the left of the fence of Frodsham Golf Course. Although there is no waymarker at this point, corner right, with the fence. A short distance beyond, the path loses height dramatically as it descends Abraham's Leap into Dunsdale Hollow where high sandstone cliffs on the right are pitted with caves resulting from erosion by wind, rain and frost. Walkers interested in etymology will be delighted to learn that "Dunsdale Hollow" interprets as "Valley of Dung".

By the waymarker post at the foot of Abraham's Leap turn left. Almost immediately there is a stile on the right which is waymarked, but not with the Sandstone Trail logo. Do not be tempted by it. Prefer, instead, the main path which continues, still downhill, to the waymarker post at the foot of Jacob's Ladder, a staircase path carved out of the rock face.

Today this dangerous exit from Dunsdale Hollow is avoided. By the waymarker post turn right for some 50 metres before turning left for a steep ascent of a flight of steps with a convenient handrail on which someone has carved the words, "Not So Far Now".

From the top of these steps the path levels as it runs along the cliff to a stile providing access to the golf course. Taking your line of direction from a waymarker and aiming to the right of a solitary gorse bush, cross the links to a narrow hedged corridor and the final stile. Continue a further few metres to Simons Lane and make a right turn to your starting point. When ready, drive into the centre of Frodsham for that well-earned afternoon tea.

Walk 5: Delamere Forest

Route	Delamere Station - Eddisbury Hill - Roman Road - King's Chair - Eddisbury Lodge - Visitor Centre - Delamere Station
Start	Delamere railway station. Map reference SJ556703
Distance	4 miles
Map	OS Explorer 267, Northwich & Delamere Forest
Getting there by public transport	Delamere railway station is served by frequent daily (including Sunday) trains from Chester, Stockport, Northwich and Manchester
Getting there by car	Delamere railway station is off the B5152 road from the A556 at Abbey Arms to Frodsham. There is a large car park on the picnic site

The Tea Shop

The Station House Café is situated in the former station house at Delamere railway station and is, not surprisingly, decorated with railway memorabilia. Because the station is still operational you can enjoy your repast as the trains come to a halt on their way to Chester or Manchester

Its scones, with lavish helpings of cream and accompanied by generous servings of tea, are a delight. So, too, are the afternoon teas: regular items include lemon meringue pie, Bakewell tart and chocolate & pear sponge. Portions are very generous. On the savoury side, the café also serves a good range from light snacks to full meals. And, as a change from tea, try the hot chocolate – one self-confessed chocaholic described it as "divine"!

Opening hours: Daily, 9.30am to 5.00 p.m; Tel: 01606 889825

Delamere Forest

When the Normans arrived in this part of Cheshire the great Forest of Mara and Mondrum, "The Forest of the Meres", covered the land between the Mersey and Nantwich. It was established as a Royal Hunting Forest and remained in use as such until the reign of Charles I.

During that period all the remaining deer were culled and, in later centuries, the great oaks were used for the building of warships. During the mid nineteenth century it was replanted but the seed used proved to be of poor quality.

After the First World War it was taken over by the Forestry Commission and coniferous species planted to maximise timber production. These included Scots and Corsican Pines, Larch and Western Hemlock.

In more recent years, in accordance with changing policy, it has been developed as a recreational amenity which has resulted in the planting of more broadleaved trees, and the provision of car parks, picnic areas, a Visitor Centre and an educational service.

The forest itself now covers 785 hectares and provides a habitat for numerous birds, including several birds of prey, insects on the meres and such mammals as fox and badger.

The Forest Visitor Centre opening times are: Mondays to Fridays, 10.30am to 12.30pm and 13.00pm to 4.15p.m; Saturdays and Sundays, 10.30am to 4.45pm.

Eddisbury Hill

This is the site of the most complex hill fort in Cheshire. Constructed by an Iron Age community, its seven acres were surrounded and defended by a wooden palisade. Demolished by the Romans, it was briefly restored to life by Queen Ethelfleda, daughter of King Alfred, during the Saxon period of our history.

The Route

Exit the car park and picnic site by passing to the right of the Station House Café and proceeding along the station approach until meeting the B5152, Station Road.

Turn right and, using the pavement, walk in the direction of the A556, initially passing a golf course on your left. Soon this gives way to a panorama of open country while on your right is a succession of bungalows.

After almost a mile turn right into Eddisbury Hill for a steep climb. As soon as the houses are left behind the extensive panorama reveals the vastness of the Cheshire Plain and the Mersey Valley. On a clear day the West Pennine Moors north of Bolton are visible.

On approaching the summit of Eddisbury Hill the land is decorated by gorse and the trees house a noisy rookery. In time the going levels and you pass a white house on the right which carries the date of 1911 along with the royal coat of arms and the initials "GR".

Walk 5 Delamere Forest

Delamere Forest

A short distance beyond, Eddisbury Hill forms a junction with Stoney Lane. Maintain direction to a stile adjacent to a gate and a footpath sign.

Take the wide, sandy track which, according to the map, follows the route of a Roman road as it keeps along the edge of the field. Beyond the fence on your immediate right is a gathering of TV masts on the summit of Pale Heights. Following a very gradual loss of altitude there is an attractive valley running off to the right but this is not on our route.

Instead, negotiate a facing stile alongside a gate before continuing to the left of a row of Scots Pines. This is followed by another gentle climb to a stile in the right-hand corner of a field. Over that, the path keeps to the left of some hawthorns and to the right of a barbed wire fence while, only a short distance below to your left, traffic roars along the A556, the Manchester to Chester road.

Following another stile maintain direction through a small plantation for 100 metres to a footpath finger post by a T-junction. Turn right along the Sandstone Trail so that you are walking in a northerly direction.

The rise on your right is Hangingstone Hill while to your left, but no longer visible, is a quarry known as King's Chair from where stone was quarried for the construction of Vale Royal Abbey.

The good, clear path enters Nettleford Wood for a delightful slightly rising stretch to a three-armed footpath post. Ignore the path heading left and signed to Yeld Lane, opting rather to stay forward with the path signed to Barnsbridge Gates.

Negotiate a stile by a gate which provides access onto a grassy path which descends gradually through an avenue of trees with distant views of Ellesmere Port and Stanlow.

As you keep "Eddisbury Lodge Cottage" on your right, the rate of descent quickens to an intersection in front of "Eddisbury Lodge". Following the sign to Delamere Station, turn right along a broad track which clings to a well-maintained holly hedge on the left as it wends its way along level ground before passing to the right of the Forestry Enterprise Visitor Centre and to the left of the Forestry Office.

On reaching a railway bridge on the left stay forward but, after a further 100 metres, turn left through a small metal gate, descend the steps and then turn right to walk through the picnic area to the car park from where you started and the Station House Café.

Walk 6: Blakemere

Route	Blakemere - Sandiway - Cockpit Lane - Daleford Manor - Newchurch Common - Whitegate Way - Kennel Bridge - Nunsmere - Blakemere
Start	Blakemere Centre on the A556. Map reference SJ598703
Distance	5 miles
Map	OS Explorer 267, Northwich & Delamere Forest
Getting there by public transport	There are frequent daily (including Sunday) buses to Sandiway from Northwich and Chester. There are buses from Altrincham on Sundays
Getting there by car	The Blakemere Centre is by the A556, between the village of Sandiway and the junction of the A49 Warrington to Whitchurch road. Large car park and no admission charge

The Tea Shop

Conveniently located within Blakemere, you'll find the Saddlers Kitchen, a light and airy café furnished with pine tables and spindle-backed chairs. Choose from teas & coffees to hot meals (homemade soup, baked potatoes and specials). For afternoon tea, there is a good range of homemade cakes plus scones, flapjacks, brownies & biscuits. Saddlers is next door to the Coach House bar & restaurant, which serves more substantial fare.

Opening Hours: All year. Monday to Sunday 9:00am to 5pm; Tel: 01606 883261.

Blakemere

The centre is housed around the cobbled courtyard of an Edwardian stable block. The redbrick buildings have been carefully and tastefully restored to accommodate a wide variety of retail units selling products from chocolates and jewellery to hand-made furniture. There is also a garden centre, aquatics centre, falconry and children's activities.

The Route

Leaving the car park strike out diagonally across the open space to the corner of the main building and, staying to the left of this, take the short footpath leading to the A556, Chester Road. Exercising caution, cross to the far side and turn right to walk eastwards along the pavement for approximately half a mile passing through a part of Sandiway village.

Beyond the traffic lights, and by the far corner of the wooden boundary fence of Sandiway Grange, now a residential home for the elderly, turn right into Cockpit Lane, a name which conjures up bygone rural entertainment. It is signed to Petty Pool and Daleford Lane.

Beyond a small clutch of large houses the surface ends, the track enters woodland, keeping just inside the boundary. Immediately beyond a Portakabin on your right, and before a set of double iron gates, turn right over a waymarked stile and then immediately left as the path skirts a skid pan used by the Cheshire Constabulary when training drivers.

After 20 metres negotiate a second stile and turn right to walk alongside a fence on your right. There is a stream down below on your left. Immediately beyond a (currently) decrepit metal gate on your right, look out for a waymark on the gatepost. Turn right and stay to the left of the

Saddlers Kitchen

wire fence for a few metres before corkscrewing left down through some trees to a stile which provides access to Daleford Lane.

Cross directly into a lane signed as a footpath to Kennel Lane. Keep the brick built Daleford Cottage on your left as you advance to a three-armed footpath post. Bear left, with the lane, to pass through Daleford Manor Caravan Park to reach Daleford Farm.

Continue with the track as it winds its way across open farmland to pass through the yard of Swallow Farm with its noisy pair of guard dogs until reaching a T-junction a few metres beyond.

Turn left along Kennel Lane as it heads eastwards through flanking holly trees. Soon, however, a large lake, created from abandoned sand workings, appears on the left. Continue until reaching a junction on the edge of Newchurch Common. Turn right so that you have another lake on your left and proceed to a waymarked stile after 30 metres. Maintain the same line of direction through some conifers.

Corner round the lake until reaching a stile in the fence on your right. Climb this onto the Whitegate Way, another of Cheshire's abandoned railway lines converted into a walking route.

Turn right, heading in a westerly direction across heathland dotted with innumerable pools with names such as "Shemmy Moss" and "Reeking Hole".

After more than a mile pass beneath Kennel Bridge to find Nunsmere, with Nunsmere Hall beyond, on your left. On approaching a second bridge, turn right up the flight of steps, to join the A49, Whitchurch to Warrington road. Turn right along this for approximately 500 metres to the traffic lights at the junction with the A556. Turn right and then, right again, along the path into the Blakemere Craft Centre.

Walk 7: Cotebrook

Route	Cotebrook - Little Budworth Common - Country Park - White Hall - Hawkswood - Beech Road - Coach Road - Hunter's Lodge - Cotebrook
Start	Cotebrook Shire Horse Centre. Map reference SJ571655. Car park shared with the Alvanley Arms - ask permission to park before starting your walk (see below for alternative start)
Distance	3¼ miles
Map	OS Explorer 267, Northwich & Delamere Forest
Getting there by public transport	Cotebrook is served by daily (not Sunday) buses from Chester, Tarporley and Bunbury. There is one bus a day from Northwich on Tuesdays, Fridays and Saturdays
Getting there by car	Cotebrook is on the A49 between Sandiway and Tarporley. Parking is restricted. An alternative start is from the car park at Little Budworth Country Park, map reference SJ593654. This is located on the Coach Road which leaves the A49 north of Cotebrook and is signed to Little Budworth. The car park is opposite the entrance to Oulton Park

The Tea Shop

Cotebrook Shire Horse Centre is set in 50 acres of Cheshire countryside, complete with picnic area, and a great place to visit before or after your walk. Home of the internationally renowned Cotebrook Stud they have been breeding prize-winning shires here for over 30 years. They have also stocked the park with a fantastic selection of British animals and birdlife, both wild and domesticated, including many rare breeds. The Lakeside Café is pleasantly situated and is open to non visitors. Accompaniments to morning coffee and afternoon tea include toasted teacakes, scones, muffins and locally made cakes. At lunchtime, choose from ploughman's lunch, jacket potatoes and paninis.

Walk 7 Cotebrook

To Sandiway

A49

N

To Kelsall

B5152

Hawkswood Farm

White Hall Farm

Budworth Pool

Little Budworth Country Park

S

Coffee House

Cotebrook

P

Little Budworth

A49

To Tarpoley

Motor Racing Circuit

Oulton Park

Oulton Lake

0   500m

Opening hours: All year 10.00am to 5.00pm (every day except Tuesdays). Admission (in 2005): Adult £7.00, Concessions £6.00, Child £5.00, Family 2 + 3 children £22.95, Under 5 free. Tel: 01829 760506.

Alternative if Shire Horse Centre full or closed: Cotebrook Coffee Shop is about 500 yards north on the A49 from the Shire Horse Centre. This serves a range of goodies from toasties to baguettes and crêpes to hot meals. Tel: 07792 254755.

Little Budworth

The thatched cottages of this tiny out-of-the-way village surround the church with its medieval tower and gargoyles. The interior is mainly of Georgian design and houses various memorials to the Egerton family which lived at Oulton Park, now the motor racing circuit.

The woodlands outside the village are remnants of the hunting Forest of Mara and Mondrum which stretched from Frodsham to Nantwich. Our route crosses what is regarded as the finest example of lowland heath in Cheshire, noted for its woodcock, brown hare, butterflies, slippery jack fungus and damselflies.

Cotebrook derives its name from the Anglo-Saxon for an enclosure or fold for animals besides the brook.

The Route

From the Shire Horse Centre, turn right out of the car park and head northwards along the busy A49 for approximately 500 metres. Pass the coffee shop mentioned on the previous page and continue for a further 100 metres until you reach a telephone kiosk, where you branch off to the right over a stream into a narrow hedged lane which climbs for a further 150 metres before levelling out.

After a quarter of a mile this lane forms a T-junction with another. Ignore the junction. Instead make a right turn over a stile by a footpath finger post onto a field path signed to Little Budworth village.
Aim for the obvious stile in the facing hedgerow some 50 metres distant. Over that veer right up a slight rise and, on gaining the crown of a very large field, strike out for the stile which stands by a gateway and close to the corner of a hedge.

Beyond that, walk to the left of another hedgerow to a stile by a metal gate. In the ensuing field remain to the left of the hedge to reach a stile adjacent to a single metal gate.

Using the waymark as the direction finder, curve a little to the left following a very obvious path to a stile alongside a wooden gate. This permits an exit onto a bridleway. Cross to the facing stile with a footpath sign.

Over this particular stile turn sharp right as the path weaves its course through the woodlands of Little Budworth Common. At the first intersection of paths keep the same line of direction until meeting a waymarked post. This is quickly followed by a T-junction.

Turn left to cross a small expanse of heathland to another intersection. This time stay forward, cross a bridleway but, at the next T-junction turn right. Then, almost immediately, go left onto a short path leading to the Coach Road. Cross this into the car park of Little Budworth Country Park.

A short digression of a hundred metres to the right will be rewarded by a view of the impressive classical main entrance to Oulton Park set against a backdrop of equally impressive beech trees. Exit the car park by taking the path to the right of the display panel. Wander through this remnant of the ancient Forest of Mara and Mondrum while keeping just inside the woodland boundary.

After some distance, pass to the right of a wooden gate to emerge onto a large area of heathland. Traverse this by following the clear path as it maintains the same line of direction, eventually crossing the metalled

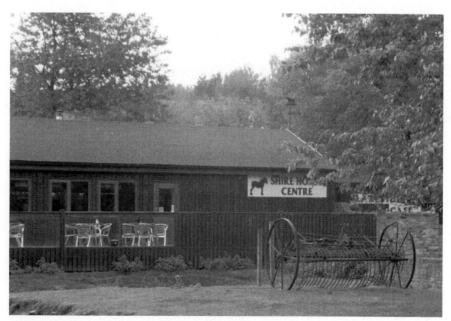

The Shire Horse Centre

driveway leading to White Hall, a large redbrick and black and white building through the trees to your right.

On meeting a bridleway, a short distance beyond, turn right. At the junction by a set of two gates, make an acute turn to your left along a path signed to the Coach Road.

At the subsequent intersection in the middle of the woodland turn right. A Y-junction is reached after only a short distance. Fork right onto a broad path which dips as it passes a pool on your left before climbing to a stile. Having negotiated this, pass through the yard of Beech House Farm to emerge onto Beech Road. Turn left. To your right is "Hawkswood", a large cream-coloured house.

Pass another small car park on your left before reaching the Coach Road. Cross into the facing bridleway and, ignoring all paths leading off to right or left, follow the lane until well beyond Hunter's Lodge.

Where the lane bends round through ninety degrees to the right by a four-armed finger post, stay forward into the sunken country lane signed to Cotebrook. This forms part of the outward route so retrace your steps to the A49 where a left turn will lead to the Coffee Shop at Cotebrook. Stop for refreshments here or turn left to continue to the Shire Horse Centre.

Walk 8: Tarporley

Route	Tarporley - Cobbler's Cross - Portal Golf Course - Eaton - Lightfoot Lane - Oakland - Hill Farm - Heath Green - Forest Road - Tarporley
Start	Car park behind the British Legion Club, Tarporley. Signed from the centre of Tarporley. Map reference SJ555624
Distance	5¼ miles
Map	OS Explorer 267, Northwich & Delamere Forest
Getting there by public transport	Tarporley is served by frequent buses daily (including Sundays) from Chester, Nantwich, Newcastle-under-Lyme and Hanley
Getting there by car	Tarporley (now by-passed) stands at the junction of the A49 Warrington to Whitchurch road with the A51 Chester to Nantwich road. Car park is signed from the main road through the village

The Tea Shop

The No. 6 Coffee Shop in Tarporley's High Street is a meeting place for locals and visitors alike. It has a plain, uncluttered atmosphere with a tiled floor and brick-faced servery. Decorations take the form of wheatsheaves and dried-flower arrangements.

The olde-world atmosphere of Tarporley's coaching past is maintained with toasted muffins on the menu. The proprietor, Carol Duncan, provides Welsh Rarebit made to her own recipe, all-day breakfasts, toasted sandwiches, sandwiches, baguettes, and soup and roll in addition to an extensive range of home-made cakes and gateaux. A range of coffees and speciality teas is available.

Opening hours: Monday to Friday, 9.30am to 5.00pm; Saturday 10.00am to 5.00pm; Sunday, 11.00am to 5.00pm; Tel: 01829 732021

Tarporley

When mentioned in Domesday Book as "Tarpolei", the village occupied a site close to the present by-pass, moving to its present location as the township flourished and developed into a market town, after receiving its first charter from Edward I.

In Burton Square, just north of Forest Road, you will find "Quarry Cottage", the only reminder that a quarry was once worked at this spot. It was here that the 15-inch footprint of an amphibian was discovered in the stone, proof that this could have been Jurassic Park.

Tarporley's heyday came with the coaching era when several of its hostelries provided accommodation for travellers between Chester and London including Celia Fiennes, that inveterate wanderer and ancestor of Sir Ranulph Fiennes. Its most famous coaching inn is The Swan, which still stands in the High Street. It is the home of the Tarporley Hunt Club probably the oldest in the country. Until 1939 the village was also the venue for race meetings and a well-salted meat pie designed to encourage thirst was traditionally served under the large chestnut tree near the Rising Sun pub.

The No. 6 Coffee Shop

Walk 8 Tarporley

To Sandiway

A49

Luddington Hill

N

Golf Course

Lightfoot Lane

Eaton

To Chester

A51

Portal Hotel & Golf Club

Golf Course

Royal Lane

Tarporley

Wettenhall Brook

0   500m

A49

A51

To Whitchurch

To Nantwich

Although Tarporley has some splendid black and white buildings dating from Tudor times, the overall impression of the High Street is Georgian. St Helen's Church dates from the fourteenth century but was extensively restored in the nineteenth. It contains memorials to two local families, the Crewes and the Dones.

The Route

Leaving the car park by the entrance turn right into High Street. Proceed a few metres beyond the Post Office. Turn right into Park Road which is signed to the hospital.

It climbs gently to pass the hospital and Rathbone Park, a complex of newly built retirement homes. A few metres beyond these, where the road bends round to the right and by a school sign, stay forward through an old gateway onto a wide track.

After 10 metres negotiate a stile and continue along the same line of direction while remaining to the immediate right of the headland separating two large fields and passing a redundant stile by a large tree.

On arriving at a large brown house on your right, negotiate a small metal gate followed by a hedged path for 20 metres to emerge onto a narrow road at Cobbler's Cross.

Turn left for approximately 100 metres and, at the point where the road bend straightens out, fork right up an unsigned lane. Pass to the right of Arderne Hall to reach a stile after 150 metres.

Climb the short path cobbled with red sandstone sets before forking left to gain a T-junction. Turn right along the surfaced track which runs across Portal Golf Course, named after the farm which once occupied the site of the rather splendid club house.

Pass the goods entrance to the Club House and stay forwards until meeting a four-armed footpath post. Turn right to follow the track signed to Eaton as it sweeps round to the left of the Club House and Flaxyard Farm before progressing through an avenue of trees with views across the Cheshire Plain to the Peckforton and Bickerton Hills.

100 metres before a large sandstone bungalow with a white gate to its right, leave wide track by diverting right towards an obvious small ladder stile with an accompanying footpath finger post.

Exercising extreme caution, because there is a blind bend a few feet to the right, cross the road to a facing stile with another footpath sign adjacent. Over that stay to the right of a hedge to a ladder stile after 50 metres. Maintain your line of direction to another stile built in the traditional style.

Beyond this cling to the right of the hedge until approximately 70 metres beyond a metal gate on your left. Then negotiate a stile on the left before taking a line diagonally right, aiming for another stile, this time at the end of a rather thin looking hedge.

Over that turn left for 20 metres and then, by a gateway, turn right over another stile before turning left to traverse a very large field. Head for the gap between the end of a row of houses to the left and a small detached redbrick cottage to the right.

Between the two is a stile which provides access to a very narrow road. Turn left along this, passing the 30 mph signs after 10 metres and the Eaton village school to your right.

At the first junction stay forward into Edgewell Lane, lined mainly with modern property although "Well Cottage", a thatched, timber-framed, black and white house stands on your left. There is a similar style house almost directly opposite and both are not only attractive but are typical of the vernacular architecture of this particular area of central Cheshire.

At the subsequent T-junction make a right turn into Royal Lane to reach the sandstone cross with its eye-catching floral decorations in the centre of Eaton village.

Ignore Sapling Lane. However, opposite another thatched white house, "Silver Birches", stands an almost inconspicuous brick house. Over the front door is a stone tablet designed to resemble an open book. It reads,

> *"God Is Truth*
> *The Word Is Truth*
> *The Spirit Is Truth*
> *Love Is Truth"*

By the far corner of this house make a left turn into Lightfoot Lane. Although there is neither nameplate or sign at this junction, Lightfoot Lane is shown on the Ordnance Survey map.

Initially it climbs fairly steeply and the surface terminates by Knowl House. Beyond a conspicuous pair of locked lapwood gates it develops into a sunken lane as it ascends between hedgerows and with a surface of sandstone bedrock which, in turn, gives way to grass.

Oak, rowan, holly, ivy and bramble indicate that the hedgerows are of ancient origin suggesting that this may once have been an old packhorse route used for the transportation of salt. There is also an abundance of wild flowers in spring when wild garlic and celandine are to be seen while in summer it is the turn of foxglove, ragged robin, red campion and the ubiquitous rosebay willowherb.

The lane continues its upward course but the gradient eases before it reaches a T-junction. The lane leading off to the right heads for the Triangulation Pillar on Luddington Hill at 145 metres above sea level. Ignore this turn and the waymarks pointing to it. Instead turn left to emerge, within 100 metres, by the 9th tee of Oaklands Golf Course.

Stay with the wide sandy track to enjoy easy walking and an extensive vista across the north Cheshire Plain to your right. The occasional bench with a litter bin adjacent provides an ideal spot for a coffee break.

After a considerable distance over the golf course this track reaches the A49 by a metal gate. Turn left along the pavement. After 300 metres turn left down a side road signed to Tarporley. However, after a mere 20 metres, make a right turn into a lane to the immediate left of a gate and running parallel to the A49.

Stay to the right of a barn before losing height to a small metal gate with a bridleway sign adjacent. This provides access to a metalled lane which is closed-off to your immediate right by a set of bollards.

Turn left along this narrow road, Heath Green, soon passing Hill Farm on your right. Where the farm boundary fence ends, and by a footpath sign reading, "Forest Road, Utkinton Road", turn right over a stile.

Stay to the left of a fence to reach a stile in the far right-hand corner of the field. Then stay to the right of a row of large trees to a waymarked stile in the left-hand field corner. Do not be tempted by a stile some 50 metres to the right of this because it provides access only to a private garden.

Over the stile turn left as directed by the waymark, walking along the boundary of a cultivated field to a stile in the corner and then maintaining the same line to the right of a hedge with a view of the Welsh Hills to the west.

The path leads alongside "Lime House" to a stile adjacent to a metal gate. Turn right along Forest Road to meet High Street after 200 metres. Turn left for the walk through the village to your starting point, pausing for that afternoon tea in the Number 6 Coffee House on your way.

Walk 9: Higher Burwardsley

Route	Cheshire Workshops - Willow Hill Farm - Sandstone Trail - Bulkeley Hill - Sarra Lane - Cheshire Workshops
Start	Cheshire Candle Workshops, Higher Burwardsley. Map reference SJ523565
Distance	3 miles
Map	OS Explorer 257, Crewe & Nantwich
Getting there by public transport	Burwardsley Post Office is served by daily buses from Chester, Whitchurch and Malpas. No Sunday service
Getting there by car	The Cheshire Workshops are signed from the A49 at Beeston and the A41 at Milton Green

The Tea Shop

Chandlers Resturant is a self-service café within the Cheshire Workshops complex. Anyone completing this walk by midday will be able to enjoy a bowl of hot, tasty soup accompanied by a crusty roll and followed by a light meal or salad. For the afternoon caller there are the usual scones, jam and tea, plus a large choice of tempting cakes.

Opening hours: Daily (including Sunday) 10.00am to 3.00pm; Tel: 01829 770401.

Cheshire Workshops

Higher Burwardsley, a straggling village of stone cottages set on the flanks of the picturesque Peckforton Hills in central Cheshire, is the home of the Cheshire Candle Workshops. Founded in a small cottage in 1974 by Bob and Anne Sanderson, they moved to larger premises in 1978 but a disastrous fire in 1980 virtually gutted the building. Within a year, however, the new workshops had risen, phoenix-like from the ashes to become one of the most popular tourist attractions in the county. In 1987 a change of ownership resulted in a new emphasis. While Richard James perpetuated the candle-making side of the business he introduced new crafts including glass blowing, pottery decoration and jewellery making. It proved enormously successful, attracting in excess of 200,000 visitors a year. New management took over in December 1994 and the business continues to grow.

Visitors can watch demonstrations of candle making and even try their own hand at the craft. These are not the simple white sticks but elaborately shaped and highly decorated artistic creations, so beautiful that it seems like sacrilege to light one.

Opening hours: Daily (including Sunday) 10.00am to 5.00pm.

The Route

Leaving the Candle Workshops car park by the official exit turn left along the narrow road for a few metres. Opposite "The Pheasant" and by a telephone kiosk, make an acute turn to the right, climbing a short, steep hill to reach a cross roads at the top.

Stay forward, even though there is a sign indicating that this road is a cul-de-sac. The gradient quickly levels out and the Cheshire Workshops appear on the far side of a field a hundred metres or so to the right.

Continue for approximately a quarter of a mile but, where the road bends sharply by the entrance to the driveway leading to Willow Hill Farm, stay with the surfaced lane by going round to the left.

After a short climb and by Fowler's Bench and Fowler's Lane, turn right, following the lane as it climbs yet again while opening-up a fine view over the plain towards the Welsh hills.

The surfaced lane terminates by the imposing red sandstone gate-house to Peckforton Castle. There, join the Sandstone Trail by turning right along the bridleway signed to Bulkeley Hill. The wide track passes between a stone wall on the right and mixed woodlands of birch, oak, beech and rowan on the left.

After a few hundred metres and by a footpath sign, turn left onto a steep, stepped path which initially has a hand rail on the right-hand side. Let the waymarks guide you as you climb steeply, twisting and turning for about half a mile through the woods which have an under storey of bracken, bramble and bilberry.

The summit of Bulkeley Hill is blessed with some fine specimens of oak and beech. The obvious path curves round the outside edge of this tree lined plateau before passing through a gateway in an old metal fence and then to the right of a fire hydrant and to the left of a small concrete building.

Beyond these landmarks the path loses altitude to a gate with a smaller metal one alongside on the boundary of the woodland.

Once through the gate swing right, as advised by the Sandstone Trail sign, following the well-trodden path over a field while staying a few metres to the right of a pylon.

Leave the field by an official gap to join Coppermine Lane. Cross into the facing lane which is signed to Rawhead Farm. A few metres before reaching "The Bungalow", with its barking dogs, and where the lane makes a sharp left turn towards Rawhead Farm, turn right over a stile to follow the path signed to Burwardsley.

Stay to the right of a wire fence which surrounds a small paddock. By the far corner of this, turn left over a waymarked stile and, keeping the fence on your left, descend a cultivated field. Pass beneath two lines of overhead wires before reaching a stile with a footpath sign. The attractive formation of Raw Head is clearly visible to your left.

Beyond the stile maintain direction, guided by the arm of the footpath finger post and also by the line of white posts erected by the farmer after removing hedgerows. In doing so you will pass to the left of a redundant stile and a large concrete water trough.

Over the next stile pass through a belt of trees some 50 metres wide to a footbridge. At the far end, turn left and then right and using the

Meshach Cottage

waymarks as direction finders, pass along the shallow valley staying just to the right of a stream until gaining another stile after some 200 metres.

This provides an exit onto Sarra Lane. Turn left up the hill before the lane levels to reach a T-junction opposite St John's Church. Turn right so that the church is on your left. Beyond Cheshire County Council's Field Study Centre the road dips into a hollow before climbing to pass "Aqueduct Cottage" on your left and the tree-covered slopes of Willow Hill on your right.

At the following road junction turn right. Along this stretch of road are three of the most unusually named cottages in Cheshire. They are "Bel Shazar", "Shadrach" and "Meshach". Another building of note is the tiny Methodist Church which was built of red sandstone in 1843.

At the subsequent junction make a right turn into the car park of the Cheshire Candle Workshops.

Walk 10: Beeston and Peckforton

Route	Beeston Castle - Moathouse Farm - Stanner Nab - Peckforton Castle - Peckforton Hall - Spurstow - Beeston Moss - Beeston Castle
Start	Car park, Beeston Castle. Map reference SJ541592. Pay & Display
Distance	7 miles
Map	OS Explorer 257, Crewe & Nantwich
Getting there by public transport	Buses daily to Beeston village from Chester, Tarporley and Nantwich. (Not Sundays)
Getting there by car	Beeston Castle is well-signposted from the A49 Warrington to Whitchurch road at Beeston Lock, about two miles south of Tarporley

The Tea Shops

Though there is no tea shop at Beeston Castle, there are two nearby (and contrasting) alternatives:

Flavours Café in Beeston Brook: Previously known as the Lock Gate café, Flavours is located on the A49, just south of Tarporley. From Beeston Castle, head east for about a mile, turn left on the A49 and you'll find the café just where the main road crosses the canal. Though fairly basic, it's a welcoming place with a surprisingly wide range of breakfast items, snacks of all sorts, hot meals (with chips and peas!) and home-made dishes including chicken curry and chilli con carne. To go with morning coffee or afternoon tea there are some excellent cakes and scones – all home-made. Open every day 8.00am to 3.30pm. Tel: 01829 732708.

The Brasserie at Peckforton Castle: Just a mile south of Beeston Castle, there's Peckforton Castle – now a luxury hotel and conference venuw. This is where to go for a touch of luxury – a rare experience on a tea-shop walk. You might look and feel a bit out of place in mud-spattered walking gear, so perhaps take a change of clothing ... and, depending on your culinary tastes, maybe your credit card too! But don't let this put you off, because a visit to the castle is a real treat. The brasserie was created from the castle's old scullery and nowadays you can have anything from a quick coffee to a full meal. With morning coffee, you might fancy a croissant or, to set you up for the day, a triple chocolate flapjack. Lunchtime treats include tempting hot or cold sandwiches, panini, and platters of meat or cheese, "large enough for two to share". In the afternoon, choose a pastry to go with one of the range of teas on offer or, for a special treat, choose their classic Afternoon Tea with sandwiches, scone, cakes and clotted cream. And, for a really special treat, all of that plus champagne and strawberries! Open every day 9.30am to 10.00pm. Tel: 01829 260930.

Peckforton Castle

Seen from a distance, the battlements of Peckforton Castle standing above the trees, give it the appearance of a fairytale castle that we all dream about. In reality it is the nineteenth century creation of John Tollemache, MP for Cheshire, who was elevated to the peerage as Baron Tollemache in 1876. Designed by Anthony Salvin, it was built of local stone between 1844 and 1851.

It was described by Sir Gilbert Scott as "The largest and most carefully and learnedly executed Gothic mansion of the present day. It is not only a castle in name but it is a real and carefully constructed medieval

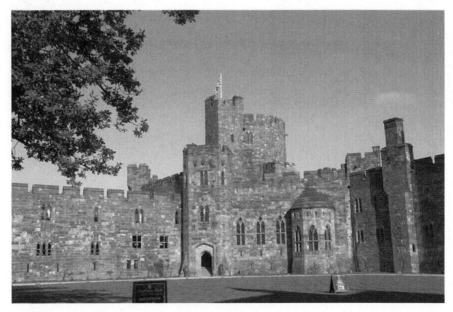

Peckforton Castle

fortress, capable of standing a siege from an Edwardian army." It was used for the filming of "Robin Hood, Prince of Thieves". For further details, see **http://en.wikipedia.org/wiki/Peckforton_Castle**

Beeston Castle

Standing on top of a crag high above the Cheshire plain, Beeston Castle enjoys a commanding position with views of the Welsh hills, the Pennines and even the Wrekin in Shropshire. The present castle dates from the thirteenth century when it was built by Ranulf, Earl of Chester, to protect his lands from the marauding Welsh.

It later passed into the ownership of the Crown and was used to house prisoners captured during the Welsh wars. It was thought impregnable until captured from the Roundheads by a group of Royalists during the Civil War. Today it is in the care of English Heritage, its extensive ruins being well worth a visit either before or after the walk.

Opening hours: 1st April to 31st October, daily, 10.00am to 6.00 p.m; 1st November to 31st March, daily, 10.00am to 4.00pm.

Beeston Castle entrance

Walk 10 Peckforton

The Route

From the car park facing the entrance to Beeston Castle turn left along the narrow road but, after some 50 metres and where the road bends to the left, stay forward, keeping to the right of the picnic area.

Pass the Sandstone Trail notice board to a through stile waymarked with the logo of the Trail, a letter "S" on the sole of a walking boot. Continue for 100 metres with the boundary wall of the castle on your right and a hedge on your left. At the first Y-junction fork left, as signed, losing altitude through the woodland which consists principally of pine trees. At the bottom of the slope a stile provides access to Wickson Lane.

Cross diagonally left to a path signed to Grindley Brook. Keeping "Tabernacle Cottage" on your right, follow the wide path across the field while enjoying some excellent walking on a sandy surface which is gentle on the feet.

Cross the wooden footbridge spanning a tiny stream followed, after 20 metres, by a stile. Maintain direction across another field until gaining a stile with a footpath finger post alongside pointing the Sandstone Trail towards Bulkeley Hill.

Turn right along the private road to pass firstly Moathouse Barn and then, secondly, Moathouse Farm, both on your right. 150 metres beyond the latter, and by a small sandstone cottage, veer left up a wide track, still signed as a stretch of the Sandstone Trail. This climbs steeply through the woods of the Peckforton Estate with woodpeckers drumming and wrens calling from the undergrowth beneath the oaks, hollies, beeches and rowans. Where the track bends round to the right, the going eases to allow the path to run along the contour.

Eventually, after passing through a gateway an intersection in the path network is reached. Turn left for the steep and stepped climb up the flank of Peckforton Hill to Stenner Nab, reaching a T-junction on the crest.

Turn left, as directed by a waymarker and, after 50 metres and by a footpath sign, turn right. A gradual descent follows. Pass another footpath sign and, just beyond, negotiate a waymarked gap in the fence, continuing to lose height until meeting the main driveway to the castle. Turn left, up the drive, to the castle and tea shop.

Afterwards, return down the driveway, continuing through the turreted gateway and reaching the road. Turn right but, by the far corner of "Castle Cottage" which is on your left, make a sharp left turn into a lane. Stay with this for some considerable distance until, having passed to the right of Peckforton Hall, you reach Peckforton Hall Lane by a footpath finger post.

Turn left following this narrow and quiet surfaced road into the village of Spurstow. Pass the entrance to Southcroft with its village notice board and red telephone kiosk.

A short distance beyond, at a minor cross roads, turn left into a narrow road recognised by a footpath sign indicating a path to Beeston.

Pass to the right of the Methodist Chapel, a red brick building dating from 1844. Beyond the first gateway the road develops into an unsurfaced track. Stay to the left of Haycroft Farm to a waymarked wooden stile adjacent to a metal gate. With Peckforton Castle directly ahead in the distance, advance a further 100 metres to a gate.

Do not go through. Rather, veer away from the hedge to a small clump of trees. Pass through these to another gate. Again do not pass through. Instead go to the right so that the hedge is on your left. At the far end of the field go through a gap by a holly tree and continue alongside the hedge. In the far left-hand corner of this field negotiate a wooden stile adjacent to a small wooden gate which is partially obscured by the vegetation and a hedgerow.

Over the stile, maintain the line of direction but now along a narrow hedged lane which, after the first house, acquires a surface of loose chippings. Stay with this lane until it meets a road by a footpath sign at Beeston Moss. Turn right. After 200 metres and by the far corner of two very small brick cottages and 100 metres before a very large black and white house, turn left over a wooden stile onto a path signed to Beeston and Beeston Brook.

Walk to the right of a hedgerow to a waymarked double stile in the field corner. Over either of these fork left, as indicated by a waymark, to traverse an arable field. The path is far from clear so aim for a small clump of trees roughly midway between Peckforton and Beeston Castles.

Negotiate the stile in the facing hedgerow before maintaining the same line of direction across a smaller cultivated field. After the next stile turn right, walking to the left of a hedge. Where this corners away to the right, continue forward, heading for the side of a brick house ahead.

After negotiating another stile, again with a footpath sign adjacent, cross the footbridge to gain the road. Turn right to a T-junction after 100 metres. Turn left into a road so narrow it is provided with passing places. Continue along this to another T-junction facing the wall of Beeston Castle. Make a left turn for the final 100 metres to the car park from which you started.

Walk 11: Audlem

Route	Audlem - Shropshire Union Canal - Cox Bank - Adderley Pool - Hawksmoor - Highfields Farm - Kinseyheath - Wood Orchard Lane - Sandy Lane - Audlem
Start	The car park off Cheshire Road, Audlem. Map reference SJ659437
Distance	6 miles
Map	OS Explorer 257, Crewe & Nantwich
Getting there by public transport	Audlem is served by frequent daily buses (Not Sunday) from Whitchurch and Nantwich. There is a restricted service from Crewe. On Saturdays there is a service from Hanley
Getting there by car	Audlem may be reached by the A525 from Newcastle-under-Lyme and Whitchurch and the A529 from Nantwich and Market Drayton. There is a large free car park off Cheshire Street near the village centre

The Tea Shop

The Old Priest House in Vicarage Lane is probably the most quaint of all the cafés included in this collection. The house itself is of uncertain date but has been in existence for more than 500 years according to Andrew Halliwell who has owned it since November, 1993.

There are two rooms with old-fashioned red and blue quarry tiles on the floor, circular tables with some spindle-backed chairs and a genuine old wooden-backed settle.

There is nothing old-fashioned about the fare they provide. In addition to a selection of light meals including Staffordshire Oatcakes with various fillings, and a very imaginative list of specials ranging from bangers and mash to Moroccan tagine, they serve afternoon teas with scones lavishly covered in local cream and a bewildering array of home-made cakes.

One speciality of the house is a traditional ice cream, made to their specification, which has given birth to a special ice-cream menu. Coffee and tea are freshly brewed and served in either cafétieres or large pots. It is an experience not to be missed and makes the perfect conclusion to any walk.

Opening hours: 10.00am to 5.00pm, but closed on Monday at 3pm and closed Tuesdays. Tel: 01270 811749.

Audlem

Audlem, undoubtedly one of the most picturesque villages in Cheshire, is located in the deep south of the county very close to the boundary with Shropshire. At 360 feet above sea level, it lies in the core of the county's pastoral countryside, being noted for its dairy products including Cheshire Cheese. Many of these may still be purchased in the village shops.

Formerly it was an important wharf on the Shropshire Union Canal which today caters only for pleasure craft. Nevertheless Audlem, sitting at the foot of a flight of 15 locks which carry the waterway down from the Shropshire Heights to the Cheshire Plain, is an important mooring area with canalside pubs and a canalside shop.

Audlem is very unusual, perhaps unique, in that the main roads leading away from the central square, all bear the names of the counties to which they lead – Cheshire, Staffordshire and Shropshire.

The focal point of this village or small town is the sturdy, square-towered parish church of St James the Great, built originally about 1200 but enlarged in the fourteenth century and renovated as recently as 1994.

It has several items of Tudor and Jacobean interest including the chancel roof and the pulpit. Close by the doorway is the ancient maypole crown and in the small chapel is a Roman funeral urn which has been dated between 70 and 80 AD.

Standing in front of the church is the Buttercross, built in 1733 and used by the local farmers for selling butter and cheese until

Audlem Church

1914. Audlem was granted a market charter by Edward I in 1295 and continued to hold its weekly market until the outbreak of the First World War.

The village is full of other interesting buildings and, after the walk, it is well worth while having a saunter through the streets with a guide leaflet which is available for a small charge from the Old Priest's House.

The Route

From the car park entrance turn right into Cheshire Street for the 150 metres to the village centre. The church of St James the Great, the Buttercross and the Bear Stone are all on your left.

The Bear Stone is a piece of granite, believed to have originated in Cumbria, which was carried south during the Ice Age before being deposited in Audlem. For decades it was used as a tethering post for the bears while they were baited by dogs.

By the Lord Combermere Hotel, a black and white building, turn right into Shropshire Street. After 200 metres and by the Bridge Inn, turn right, as signed, for the Wharf where a left turn down a short flight of steps leads onto the canal towpath.

Make another left turn and, with the canal on your right, pass under the bridge to emerge into a landscape which is lush, green, rolling and pastoral, the very essence of rural Cheshire. The path climbs alongside a series of locks before passing under Bridge number 77.

More locks follow, plus a milestone indicating that Nantwich is seven miles distant, Norbury Junction 16½ miles and Autherley Junction 32. Mallard and moorhen grace the water while it is not uncommon to observe a heron either flying overhead or standing motionless on the bank.

By bridge number 76 the gradient levels out while the path acquires a grass surface which is gentle on the feet. Remain with the canal, crossing the boundary into Shropshire shortly beyond the bow bridge which carries Bagley Lane overhead.

A long straight stretch carries you to Castle Hill, where formerly a Motte and Bailey castle occupied the site. A short distance beyond Pool House and Adderley Pool Bridge you approach Hawksmoor Bridge. A few metres before reaching it, however, go left up the short flight of steps and negotiate the small metal gate to make a left turn along the approach road to Hawksmoor Farm. The farmhouse is a stately, well-proportioned and elegant building in red brick.

Pass to the left of the farmhouse but continue forward through the middle of the stockyard with its enormous covered pens and two metal

Walk 11 Audlem

Audlem

A529

N

To Whitchurch

To Newcastle-under-Lyme

A525

Shropshire Union Canal

Wood Orchard Farm

Kinsey Heath

Woodhouse Farm

Woodhouse Lane Farm

Highfield Farm

Coxbank Brook

Shropshire

A529

Adderley

Hawksmoor

0   500m

gates. The concrete track soon develops into a wide unsurfaced lane flanked by hedgerows and, especially after wet weather, can be very muddy.

In due course the hedges are replaced by fencing on both sides before a metal gate signals the end of the lane. Beyond, maintain direction to the right of an electric fence, proceeding through a wide avenue of oaks while traversing a landscape resembling a parkland as the county boundary slips unnoticed under your boots.

Soon Highfields Farm which is noted for its herd of English Holsteins, comes into view a short distance away to the right. This imposing half-timbered black and white mansion is the first house in Cheshire.

Along this grassy path notice the gnarled stump of a tree on your left. It is reminiscent of a Henry Moore Sculpture except that this has been fashioned by nature.

With Highfields Farm away to your right, and by a clump of broadleaved trees, pass through an official gap in the fence to meet the wide track which comes from the farm. Turn left along this, cross a cattle grid and remain with it until reaching an inverted Y-junction recognised by a small, white-painted boulder. On it is an arrow pointing to "Floristry and Country Salon".

Turn left, proceeding along the level track until meeting Woodhouse Lane by a black and white house. Go left along the narrow road for approximately a quarter of a mile to reach a T-junction.

Turn left into Bagley Lane which is signposted to Swansbach and Market Drayton. Opposite Kinseyheath Farm and by a footpath finger post, turn right over a stile to advance to the right of the boundary fence of Kinsey House, a white affair carrying the date 1902.

Beyond the next stile, set into a facing hedge, make a direct line for the left-hand corner of the field. Turn left over the stile and then turn immediately to the right.

Walk to the left of the boundary hedge of a cultivated field, following it round the first corner. By the second corner negotiate a stile before keeping forward as directed by the waymark. Initially the path is clear and well-used as you aim for a distant house with a long row of chimney pots. However, having passed under some overhead wires, veer right towards a hedge corner and then keep a hedge on your left until the next waymarked stile by a wooden finger post.

This stile provides access to Orchard Wood Lane. Cross directly to a facing footpath sign. Keeping to the right of a tiny red brick cottage, proceed along a broad track.

Look out on your left for a giant willow rising from what was obviously a pond and, just beyond, ignore the left turn to Fields Farm. Remain along the lane until, a short distance after Sandy Lane Farm, you reach a junction. Turn left over the stile adjacent to a footpath finger post. Taking your direction from the arm of the post, cross a large field to the hedge corner on the right.

Continue to the left of this hedge to a stile. This permits access to a tiny village green, once the traditional site for a maypole. Cross it to reach Vicarage Lane opposite the tiniest house in Audlem and the rather more imposing Old Grammar School.

Now an old people's home, it is a building of the Stuart period dating from 1646 and paid for by three rich local people. It remained a grammar school until the early years of this century, re-opening as a mixed senior School in 1913 and remaining in use as an educational establishment until 1965.

Opposite the Grammar School, turn left along Vicarage Lane. Climb the short distance to the Old Priest's House and welcome refreshments before crossing the Square into Cheshire Street and returning to the car park.

Walk 12: Bridgemere

Route	Bridgemere - Phynsons Hayes - Checkley Wood - Checkley - Bank Farm - Bridgemere
Start	Bridgemere Garden World on the A51 between Nantwich and Woore. Map reference SJ725436
Distance	5½ miles
Map	OS Explorer 257, Crewe & Nantwich
Getting there by public transport	None
Getting there by car	Bridgemere Garden World is on the A51 south of Nantwich and north of Woore, approximately 100 metres north of the boundary between Cheshire and Shropshire. Large car park for patrons

The Tea Shop

Bridgemere Garden World offers an Ice Cream Parlour, Doughnut Hut and, probably of most interest, a Tea Room. Breakfasts, lunches, fresh salads, afternoon and cream teas, tempting cakes and local ice cream are available.

Opening hours: Daily, 9.00am to dusk in summer; Daily, 9.00am to 5.00pm in winter; tel: 01270 521100.

Bridgemere Garden World

John Ravenscroft launched Bridgemere Garden World in the early 1960s cultivating roses on three acres of land by the roadside. Today the centre, the largest in Britain, covers 140 acres. The nursery grows nearly a million plants a year and sells more plants in more varieties than anywhere else in Britain. As one visitor remarked, "I could easily spend a whole day there just looking at the different plants" – but we don't have time to do that and go for a walk!

The Route

Leaving Bridgemere Garden World by the car park exit, turn right along the A51 but, after 200 metres and by the far end of a brick cottage and a waymarker post, turn right again this time into a hedged lane.

Within about 300 metres, and by a footpath sign, turn right through a metal gate before bearing slightly left towards an obvious waymarker post. Stay to the right of this and also of a subsequent row of oak trees to descend to a stile in a very shallow valley.

At the far end of a wooden footbridge spanning the brook veer right through a narrow belt of trees whilst climbing gently for 15 metres to another stile.

Over that turn sharply to the right to walk along the boundary of a very large field with a wood on your immediate right. At this point the landscape is gently undulating and well-wooded with large numbers of pheasants wandering freely. In the far corner of this field negotiate a stile before bearing left, as per the waymark, to a white metal gate with a footpath sign adjacent.

Pass through the yard of Phynsons Hayes Farm and then bear left along a wide cinder track which is waymarked. In the very far distance ahead is the unmistakable outline of Mow Cop near Congleton.

Having passed through a gateway, there is a tree-lined pond on your right which boasts a large population of Mallard. From this spot on a clear day it is possible to see the Peckforton Hills and, beyond them, the Clywydian Hills of Wales.

After some considerable distance pass to the right of an elevated green fuel tank before going through a waymarked metal gate. After 100 metres there is a gas pipeline marker on your left. By this stage the lane has lost its open aspect, having acquired hedgerows of oak, hawthorn and willow on both sides. Checkley Wood is but a field's distance away to your left.

Stay with the track as it negotiates three sets of gates in quick succession and twists its way to the left of Checkley Wood Farm before acquiring a metalled surface.

After a considerable distance, and by Checkley Wood Cottages, turn left along the concrete drive leading to New Checkley Wood Farm. Stay to the left of the farmhouse but through the centre of the yard as directed by a series of waymarks and signs. After leaving the farm the track loses its surface as it runs between two lines of electric fence, erected to control the grazing of the large herds of cattle.

When the track ends stay forward across the centre of the very large field while aiming for some distant cottages and passing by a wooden waymarker post standing by zinc cattle troughs on the way. On approaching, make a line for the blue gate to the right of the cottages to reach the road. Ignore the waymark which points right and is giving directions for a much longer walk. Instead make a left turn along the road through Checkley hamlet.

Checkley cottage

Look for the attractive thatched cottages and Checkley Hall as you walk through. A slight climb will bring you to a house on the left bearing a plaque which reads: "DLB 1907". By this, turn left into a narrow surfaced lane which is signed as a cul-de-sac. Pass to the right of Bank Farm and look out for "Cherry Tree Cottage" which has an old-fashioned hand pump in its garden.

100 metres beyond this, turn right over a stile but ignore the direction of the footpath arm. Rather, bear left over a cultivated field to pass close by a pylon before descending into a hollow where there is a waymarked stile. Beyond, and following the distinctive path, continue forward over the hump in the centre of a meadow to negotiate a narrow footbridge before heading up the slope to a stile alongside another footpath sign.

Advance to the second stile after six metres, cross another footbridge, negotiate the stile at the far end and then turn left. Almost immediately turn right to walk to the left of a hedge. After several metres swing right, with the path, as it passes through the hedgerow to join a lane which carries you to a waymarked stile by a metal gate.

This provides access to a lane. Turn left to pass Bridgemere Farm before, some distance beyond, re-joining your outward route back to Bridgemere Garden World.

Walk 13: Nantwich

Route	Nantwich - Welshman's Lane - Shropshire Union Canal - Green Lane - Nantwich Lake - Nantwich
Start	Nantwich Book Shop, High Street, Nantwich. Map reference SJ651523
Distance	4 miles
Map	OS Explorer 257, Crewe & Nantwich
Getting there by public transport	Nantwich Station has direct rail services from Chester, Crewe, Whitchurch, Shrewsbury, Hereford, Newport and Cardiff. Daily including Sundays. In addition to local services Nantwich has daily (including Sunday) buses from Hanley, Newcastle-under-Lyme, Crewe, Tarporley and Chester. Frequent daily buses from Audlem and Whitchurch (Not Sundays)
Getting there by car	Nantwich may be reached by the A530 from Whitchurch and Middlewich, the A529 from Audlem and Market Drayton, the A51 from Chester and Stone, the A500 from Stoke and Newcastle, the A534 from Crewe and Wrexham, and the A500 from Junction 16 on the M6 Motorway. There are several signed car parks in the town centre

The Tea Shop

The coffee lounge at the Nantwich Bookshop is centrally located in an impressive square on High Street. The timber-framed Tudor building is easy to spot and provides both a pavement café and an upstairs coffee lounge. There's a wide range of home-baked cakes, scones and other "light bites" plus salads and main meals at lunch time. Treat yourself to a cream tea or splash out on an old-fashioned afternoon tea with sandwiches, scones, clotted cream and cakes on a traditional tiered stand – maybe better at the end of a walk than the beginning. Waitress service, booking essential for the "posh" tea.

Opening hours: Monday to Saturday, 9am to 4.30pm. Tel: 01270 611665.

Nantwich

Nantwich started life as Hellath Wen, meaning "Salt Pit" before the Anglo-Saxon invasions resulted in a name change to Warmundestrou. Under the Normans it became Wich Malbanc, later changed to Namtwych which, in turn, has been corrupted into the present name.

It was salt which laid the foundations of the town's lasting prosperity from Roman times until the nineteenth century. By this time it had developed into an important market town for South Cheshire with boot and shoe manufacture and glove making adding to its wealth.

The Great Fire of 1583 lasted for 20 days, destroying much of the existing town. It also provided an excellent opportunity for re-building, towards the cost of which Queen Elizabeth I contributed. Some of the oak beams which she sent gave their name to the present Beam Street.

Often referred to as "The Cathedral of South Cheshire", because of its size, the parish church of St Mary well repays a visit. This is not the place

Nantwich Bookshop and coffee lounge

to provide a detailed description because there are numerous guides on sale within the church itself.

Many of the sixteenth century black and white buildings survive, providing Nantwich with its unique atmosphere and have led to its being classified as one of this country's 51 Town Preservation Sites. Many of the buildings are passed on this walk.

Town guides are available from the Tourist Information Centre, Market Street, Nantwich CW5 5DG. Tel: 01270 537359.

The Route

Turn left out of the bookshop and walk along High Street to Oat Market, where you turn left again to reach Water Lode. Cross directly by the traffic lights to enter Welsh Row, the street once used by Welsh cattle drovers coming into Nantwich for salt.

The Row was formerly part of the main road from London to Wales during the coaching era and was also used by the Royalist Army on its approach to Nantwich during the Civil War.

Close by the bridge over the River Weaver at the entrance to Wood Street is the site of the original salt spring which supplied salt to the Roman garrison and continued in use until the nineteenth century.

Continue along Welsh Row but, by the far corner of Grocott's Garage, turn right by a footpath sign into King's Lane, passing between fences to a stile after 100 metres. Continue forward to the right of a hawthorn hedge before veering slightly to the right to another stile which is located about 50 metres to the right of the field corner. Over that, turn through ninety degrees to the left, staying close-in to the hedge on your left and then turning right in the first field corner.

By the second field corner turn left over a small planked footbridge. At the far end turn right over a stile. Proceed to the right of a hedge and in the next corner turn right over another footbridge before advancing to a stile in another field corner.

Continue forward, still to the left of a hedge until reaching a wooden gate which provides an exit onto Welshman's Lane. Turn left along this quiet road for about 250 metres until arriving at a redbrick cottage standing where the lane bends sharply to the left. There, turn right between the black and white bollards onto a narrow path which climbs the embankment onto the towpath of the Shropshire Union Canal.

Turn left along the towpath crossing Chester Road by means of the Nantwich Aqueduct and continuing by the canal moorings where several narrow boats are tied up. Many of these have elaborate decorations and

Walk 13 Nantwich

enjoy such names as "Woven Grass", "Topas", "Peregrine" and "Elysium". There is open country to both left and right but the far bank is tree-lined. Mallard may be seen swimming while the numbers of anglers on the banks testify to the abundance of fish. There is also a view of Acton Church to the right and of Nantwich Church to the left.

Walk under the arched stone bridge carrying Marsh Lane over the canal and pass the milestone which announces, "Nantwich 1 mile, Autherley Junction 38 miles and Norbury Junction 22½ miles".

On reaching Green Lane Bridge pass underneath before making an acute left turn up the bank to Green Lane. Cross to a small metal gate alongside a five-barred one complete with a bridleway sign.

Go through the small gate and, with your back to the canal, walk to the left of a hedge. Pass to the left of a tree-surrounded pond and through another small metal gate and continue between a wooden fence on your left and a hedge on your right to a small wooden gate.

Through this cross the railway line to another small gate and maintain direction through a waymarked gate. Negotiate a small metal gate into some sheep pens and exit by a five-barred one to follow a well-maintained path which crosses a wooden footbridge before reaching the A530, a few metres to the left of Shrewbridge House.

Turn left along the main road but, after 100 metres, turn left again over an area of open grassland to a footbridge spanning the River Weaver some 50 metres from the road. At the far end turn right along the path with Nantwich Lake between you and the A530.

Beyond the far end of the lake keep to the left of a specially created wildflower meadow to the memorial to Flight Lieutenant Arthur Brown of the United States Army Air Force who, on January 14th, 1944, stayed at the controls of his Thunderbolt fighter plane to avoid crashing onto Nantwich town centre with the possibility of a major loss of life. A native of New York, he was only 23 years-old when he performed this heroic act for which the inhabitants of Nantwich will be forever grateful. From this point onwards the path acquires a surface and passes beneath the railway before reaching a T-junction. Fork right to regain the A530.

Turn left along this to the traffic island where a left fork leads into Water Lode. At the first junction make a right turn into Mill Street where several mills have stood since the one recorded in the Domesday Book of 1086.

Continue along Mill Street and bear left at the Wickstead Arms, along the pedestrianised High Street and you soon reach your starting point, Nantwich Book Shop.

Walk 14: Hassall Green

Route	Vistra Marina - M6 Motorway - Woody Fields - Malkin's Bank - Trent and Mersey Canal - Vistra Marina
Start	Vistra Marina, Hassall Green. Map reference SJ772584
Distance	3 miles
Map	OS Explorer 257, Crewe & Nantwich
Getting there by public transport	Hassall Green has daily buses (not Sunday) from Sandbach, Alsager and Hanley
Getting there by car	Hassall Green is on a minor road which is signed from the A533 south of Sandbach and from Wheelock Heath on the A534. There is a car park at the Vistra Marina, otherwise use roadside parking

The Tea Shop

Lock 57 is, as the name suggests, alongside the canal and is well patronised both by the boating fraternity and locals. There are several reasons for this, not least being the fact that the lock is about midway up the flight of thirty which elevates the Trent and Mersey Canal from the Cheshire Plain to Stoke-on-Trent. So what better place to pause for a mid-morning coffee or Afternoon Tea, sitting inside or at one of the tables on the green outside, idly watching the boats go by.

The establishment is housed in a building that dates from 1766 and served originally as a stable and hay store for horses once used for hauling the barges. It was also a shop for the Navvies who could spend their company tokens there.

The walls are red brick, and the roof is supported by thick wooden beams. The view through the windows is of the locks and the undulating Cheshire countryside with traffic roaring along the M6 Motorway only a short distance away.

Described as "Café style in the day and Brasserie by night", walkers are probably more interested in the café offerings. These include homemade scones, teacakes, flapjack and other goodies. Breakfast items are from 9.30 to 1pm. Lunch menu includes soups, salads and toasties.

Opening hours: 9.30 to 4pm, Mon - Sat and 9.30 to 5pm Sun. Dinner: Tues – Fri: 6:30pm – 11pm; Sat: 6:30pm – midnight. Tel: 01270 762266.

Hassall Green

The Route

From the Vistra Marina turn right along the road leading away from the Trent and Mersey Canal and heading towards the village of Hassall Green. At the first road junction by the "Romping Donkey" pub stay forward along the road signed to Smallwood. A small estate of houses, "The Paddock", is on your left.

At the second road junction, within 100 metres of the first, stay forward again but only for a few metres before turning left into Charles Square. Walk about 50 metres along the approach road to enter the actual square which is surrounded by houses. Cross diagonally to the left-hand corner where a signed footpath leaves the square between houses numbered 55 and 57. It reaches a stile after 50 metres.

Walk 14 Hassall Green

Beyond this take the well-defined path across the centre of the field towards the M6 Motorway. Negotiate a stile in the far corner and turn right. Stay close to the fence on your left which forms the motorway boundary. It is interesting to compare your speed with that of the traffic hurtling by. You have time to observe the landscape with its flora and fauna.

After another stile follow the same line of direction to the next before a sharp right turn brings you to Betchton Road. Turn left over the bridge spanning the motorway. Some 25 metres beyond turn right over an unsigned stile set back in the hedge and, after a mere four metres, negotiate a waymarked stile.

Cross the following field on the clearly defined path and, over the next stile which is set into a wire fence, turn left through approximately 40 degrees to an obvious waymarked stile about half way along the narrow field.

Beyond this stile continue in the same direction, still along a well-trodden path, as it skirts to the left of a wood while gradually losing height towards yet another stile after about 100 metres.

Turn right over this one, cross a wooden footbridge and, at the far side, turn sharp left as instructed by the waymark. The path now keeps to the right of a small stream as it pursues its course through a shallow valley that resembles many in the White Peak of Derbyshire, the Yorkshire Dales or the Cotswolds.

The grassland is peppered with clumps of gorse, nettle, rosebay willowherb, hawthorn, bracken and bramble while willows, oak and beech dot the gradual slopes on either side.

Stay forward over further stiles until a lane is reached. Ignore the facing stile, instead turning left as the sunken lane climbs out of the valley before regaining Betchton Road by "Woodyfields Cottage".

Turn right along the road, ignoring a footpath signed to the left, until reaching the entrance to Malkin's Bank Golf Club. Turn left into the approach road and, after only a few metres and in front of the Club House turn left onto the towpath of the Trent and Mersey canal.

Continue alongside the canal with the distinctive landmark of Mow Cop in the far distance ahead and noticing bridge number 149 which is doubled-arched to permit two way traffic.

After walking under the M6 climb slightly to a lock, turn left over the gate and then right for Lock 57.

Walk 15: Little Moreton Hall

Route	Little Moreton Hall - Boarded Barn Farm - Scholar Green - Macclesfield Canal - Old House Green - Little Moreton Hall
Start	Car park, Little Moreton Hall. Map reference SJ831589
Distance	3½ miles
Map	OS Explorer 268, Wilmslow, Macclesfield & Congleton
Getting there by public transport	None
Getting there by car	Little Moreton Hall is adjacent to and signed from the A34 approximately four miles south of Congleton

The Tea Shop

The Tea Room at Little Moreton Hall is located inside the main building and, as you would expect, has black and white interior walls and wooden beams. Bear in mind that the hall is owned by the National Trust and non-members have to pay the admission charge to get into the teashop/restaurant. NT members get in free.

It serves light lunches (salads and hot meals), sandwiches and afternoon teas with scones, cakes and delicious desserts, all of which may be accompanied by a choice of speciality teas or coffee.

Opening hours: April to October daily 11.30 to 5.00pm. But closed Mondays and Tuesdays except Bank Holidays. November to mid-December Saturdays and Sundays only 11.30 am to 4.00pm. Closed from mid-December to the end of March.

Little Moreton Hall

Dating from 1480 Little Moreton Hall has undergone few changes in its history so that it represents, better than perhaps any other building in England, the medieval type of architecture. Its striking black and white timber framed architecture, with its protruding gables, has made it a great favourite with photographers, both amateur and professional.

Little Moreton Hall

It is noted for its Long Gallery, Withdrawing Room, secret chambers, oak panelling and decorative plasterwork. Outside it is surrounded by a moat and has a very unusual Elizabethan Knot Garden. Built by the Moreton family who lived there for centuries it is now owned by the National Trust.

Opening hours (2011): mid-March to the end of October, Wednesdays to Sundays, 11.00am to 5.00 p.m; early November to mid-December and from end of February to mid-March, Saturdays and Sundays only, 11.00am to 4.30 p.m; otherwise, closed during the winter.

The Route

From the car park entrance turn left along the A34, walking in a southerly direction and using the pavement on the western side. After 150 metres, and by a footpath finger post, turn right over a stile to walk the path to the immediate right of a hawthorn hedge. After approximately 50 metres turn left over a stile set into that hedge and then turn right, passing between a fence on the left and hedge on the right.

Negotiate another stile, reached after a mere 20 metres, and veer to the right, heading for the right-hand corner of the buildings of Boarded Barn Farm. The path actually leads to a stile and waymarkers just a few metres to the right of a white bath.

With the farm on your left, advance to another waymarked stile within 30 metres and adjacent to a metal gate. Over that remain to the right of a hedge to yet another waymarked stile.

Turn left and, remaining still to the right of a hedge, aim for a footpath finger post and a small wooden gate alongside a wooden gate. Through the gate, make a right turn along the minor road which eventually leads to Rode Heath. After about a quarter of a mile it dips slightly to a redbrick bridge.

At the far end of this and by a footpath sign, make a left turn over a stile and bear left, taking your line of direction from the arm of the footpath post while aiming for a gateway in the line of trees ahead.

Climb slightly, pass through the gateway to continue to the left of a row of Scots Pines. After 120 metres go through an official gap in the facing hedge and stay forward alongside a fence on your right to a stile and sign some five metres to the left of a metal gate.

On the far side turn left along a narrow lane, crossing a footbridge after 20 metres. Proceed by two houses on your left and, ignoring a signed path to your right, stay with the lane as it widens out to reach the A34 at Scholar Green.

Cross to a facing road of about 10 metres in length. At the end go left into Station Road. Initially this is lined with houses on both sides but, beyond Stone Chair Lane, open countryside replaces the houses on the left. Mow Cop is directly ahead.

By Kent Green Farm, a large and impressive redbrick house, swing left into a surfaced lane signed as a public footpath. It is a cul-de-sac leading only to Low Farm.

Where the lane dips slightly and bends round to the left on its final approach to Low Farm, go over the stile with a faded yellow waymark on your right.

Climb gently for about 150 metres to the right of a wood before gaining a stile and the towpath of the Macclesfield Canal. Turn left along the towpath which is tree lined and offers a scene of peace and tranquillity. The elevated position of the canal provides some far-reaching views out over the pastoral landscape of South Cheshire. Often, while walking this stretch, I have seen a fox scurrying over a neighbouring field even in broad daylight.

After some distance you will pass Ramsdell Hall, an imposing mansion in the classical and Jacobean styles. Its lawns, reaching down to the water's edge, are immaculate and of a quality that would put even Oval to shame.

Stay alongside the canal, going under the arched stone bridge at Old House Green and continuing with the towpath until reaching bridge number 85, another stone arched affair. Pass beneath this and immediately turn left up a flight of a dozen stone steps as directed by a yellow waymark to emerge onto New Road. Turn right along this, pass "Keeper's Cottage" on your left and lose height round a double bend.

After approximately 250 metres, and by the entrance to the driveway to Hall Farm with its cattle grid, turn left over a wooden stile adjacent to a footpath sign. Taking direction from the arm of the post, advance across the field on a fairly clear path to pass between two pylons under two sets of overhead wires. Just beyond the pylons descend the sloping field to a wooden stile set into a gap between the trees.

Maintaining the same line of direction climb the slope, stay to the left of a few solitary trees and gradually bear left while staying to the right of a belt of trees to another wooden stile by a metal 5-barred gate. Go forward across the centre of the next large field with a canal bridge a few metres to the left.

Over this stile turn right along a wide track which runs between a fence post on the left and a hedge on the right. Stay to the left of this hedge to another stile before turning sharply to the right to walk alongside a hedge which forms the boundary of a large field.

After the stile in the far corner of the field stay alongside the hedge to another and then turn through 45 degrees to the left for the crossing of the centre of another field to the diametrically opposed corner by some farm buildings.

There, negotiate another stile by a footpath sign and walk to the left of a gate, then a fence and then a hedgerow. On the far side of these is a farm house with an ancient cruck-frame barn which is as old as Little Moreton Hall and has occupied the same site for several centuries. Remarkably it remains in very good condition and is still in everyday use.

Beyond the next stile follow the broad track to pass Little Moreton Hall on your way to the car park. However, it is well worth diverting to tour this historic building and to enjoy a cream tea at the same time.

Walk 16: Marton

Route	Church Farm - Bunce Lane - Sandpit Farm - Fern Farm - Higher Gorsley Green - Davenport Lane - Oak Lane - Church Farm
Start	Church Farm, Marton. Map reference SJ850681
Distance	4 miles
Map	OS Explorer 268, Wilmslow, Macclesfield & Congleton
Getting there by public transport	None
Getting there by car	Marton is on the A34 between Wilmslow and Congleton, about three miles south of Monks Heath. There are minor roads to Macclesfield and Holmes Chapel

The Tea Shop

The Marton Kitchen coffee shop at Church Farm is just across the road from The Davenport pub and is located within a renovated farm building. Operating under the experienced eye of Lindsay Sommer, it's a popular stop for walkers, cyclists and visitors to this pleasant part of Cheshire. The emphasis is on quality ingredients, locally sourced where possible.

At coffee or tea time, there is a choice of sandwiches, cakes, muffins and panini accompanied by a good range of teas, coffees and cold drinks. More substantial offerings range from Welsh Rarebit to curries, filled Cheshire oatcakes and, for bigger appetites, fish & chips, and "Treacle Town" pies (a reference to traditional Macclesfield specialities),

Opening hours: 10:00am to 4:30pm, Tuesday to Sunday. Tel: 01260 224344.

Marton

Church Farm is at the heart of the small village of Marton. Next to the Marton Kitchen, there's Churches Deli (handy for takeaway supplies), and there's also a beauty salon and La Popote restaurant – quite a community.

The nearby parish church of St James and St Paul is the oldest half-timbered black and white church in Europe. Founded in 1343 as a Chantry Chapel, the oldest surviving part of the building is the nave.

The Route

After visiting the church of St James and St Paul, cross the A34 to the facing stile by the footpath finger post and maintain direction over the field aiming for the corner of a hedge approximately 100 metres ahead.

From that corner remain to the left of the hedge, passing several enormous oak trees en route to a waymarked stile in the field corner. Advance some 25 metres to a second stile which permits an exit onto Bunce Lane. Turn left for 150 metres. Beyond a Z-bend and by a metal gate and footpath sign, turn right over a stile.

Walk to the left of a fence and, subsequently, of a hedge to a facing stile and, with Bunce Lane Farm a short distance to your left, cross the middle of two successive fields to a stile by a pylon in a field corner. Using the stiles and a line of overhead wires as your guide, continue forwards until passing between the house and outbuildings of Sandpit Farm which appears to specialise in the growing of garden turf.

Marton church

By the house turn left along the short drive to Messuage Lane, a narrow surfaced road. Turn right and, using the wide grass verge, proceed for about half a mile.

By the far end of Keeper's Cottage, an attractive brick building, there is a T-junction. Turn right into Hodgehill Lane which is signed to Siddington Heath.

Pass Fern farm with its barking but harmless dogs and continue for about 150 metres to the entrance to Daisy Bank Farm. By the footpath sign opposite turn right through a metal gate and bear slightly to the right for an obvious stile in the facing hedgerow some 80 metres distant.

Over this stile stay close to the hedge on your right to another stile and then bear diagonally left to a fence corner as indicated by the waymarker. There turn right so that you have a fence on your immediate right. In the next field corner turn left but, after 40 metres, go right over another stile. Advance to the left of a hedge and pass to the right of a small pond to a stile which permits access to Davenport Lane.

Turn right, soon passing Higher Gorsley Green Farm with its collection of goats and continue until, by Bank Farm, you reach the A34. Cross to the pavement and turn left. After approximately 300 metres and by a footpath sign, turn right through a gate. Staying to the right of a hedge walk to the first field corner and turn left over a waymarked stile.

Immediately turn right to another stile in a wooden fence and advance to the right of the boundary of Mere Farm. By a gate turn left over another stile and turn right along the farm drive until arriving at School Lane by a footpath sign.

Turn right but at the Y-junction by the village school, fork left into Oak Lane, following this round until it reaches the A34. Turn left and pass the Davenport Arms on your right to regain Church Farm and the Marton Kitchen.

Walk 17: Alderley Edge

Route	Alderley Edge village - Castle Rock - Armada Beacon - The Wizard - Nether Alderley Mill - Nether Alderley Church - Blackshaw Lane - Alderley Edge village
Start	Car park, Alderley Edge village. Map reference SJ844783
Distance	6½ miles
Map	OS Explorer 268, Wilmslow, Macclesfield & Congleton
Getting there by public transport	Alderley Edge station is served by trains from Manchester, Stockport, Wilmslow and Crewe. There are frequent daily (including Sunday) buses from Manchester, Wilmslow and Macclesfield
Getting there by car	The town of Alderley Edge is on the A34, some three miles to the south of Wilmslow. There are five pay and display car parks in the village centre, but note that the one on The Parade (the one with the large supermarkets) is restricted to 2 hours

The Tea Shops

The Wizard Tea Room on Alderley Edge itself, part-way round the walk, is a simple stone building adjoining the National Trust Information Centre. It is white both outside and in, the interior being decorated with various items of old farming equipment and horse harnesses. In winter it is heated by a blazing wood burning stove.

The menu embraces freshly cut or toasted sandwiches with a variety of fillings, soup of the day, toasted teacakes, delicious home-made scones with jam and cream and a selection of cakes, accompanied by coffee or one of a choice of speciality teas.

Opening hours: Saturdays, Sundays and Bank Holidays 10.00am to 5.00pm; weekday groups on request. Tel: 01625 572706.

Until early 2011, there was an excellent tea shop in Alderley Edge called "Fruitcake". Unfortunately, this has closed to make way for a Waitrose supermarket. It's possible that Fruitcake will resurface elsewhere, or maybe Waitrose will have its very own café, but there are other possibilities. Firstly, there's a branch of Costa Coffee quite near to The Parade; it doesn't have a tea shop ambience, but it is convenient.

Alternatively, about half-way along the main road (London Road), you'll find the Village Café – a blend of coffee bar and tea shop with a pleasant, modern environment. There's a good range of baguettes, panini, sandwiches and cakes (mostly home-made) on offer, together with a good range of coffees, teas and smoothies. Luckily for walkers, the café is open every day from 8am to 5pm.

Now that the Alderley Edge by-pass has been completed, it is likely that the café culture will become more established and we may see more tea shops on the high steet.

Alderley Edge

Alderley Edge is one of several sandstone escarpments rising abruptly from the Cheshire Plain. Now owned by the National Trust, it is more than 600 feet above the surrounding countryside thereby affording some extensive views over towards Kinder Scout, Bleaklow and other outstanding features within the Peak District National Park.

Copper was first mined there by the Romans, the industry continuing at intervals until it finally ceased during the nineteenth century. The mines are now closed and sealed-off from the general public but occasional guided tours are arranged by the National Trust in association with a local caving club.

Beacon Point marks the site where a bonfire was lit on the approach of the Spanish Armada in 1588, one of many such early warning signals organised in a chain throughout England to alert the local militia to be prepared in case of an invasion.

As with other sites throughout Britain, Alderley Edge is closely linked in popular mythology with King Arthur. According to one legend the king, with all the Knights of the Round Table, sleeps in one of the great caverns awaiting the time when this country once again requires their help.

The Wizard Hotel takes its name from Merlin, who, according to another popular tale, met a drunken farmer on his way home over the Edge and took him into the cavern to sell his horse to a knight who did not have one.

The village, which takes its name from this sandstone ridge, was once the home of the important Stanley Family, one of their number serving as Dean of Westminster. It developed during the nineteenth century into

Alderley Edge

a residential area for Manchester cotton magnates and business men who built the fine houses, many of which have now been converted into flats.

Nether Alderley Mill

It is known that a mill existed in Alderley as early as 1290 but no details have survived about its exact location. The present building dates from the sixteenth century and is unusual because the rear faces the embankment of the reservoir constructed to store water for driving the machinery.

It was worked by a long line of millers until the early 1940s when extensive repairs were needed. In view of the declining trade for such mills, the cost of saving it was prohibitive and a decision was taken to close it down.

After the Second World war it was given to the National Trust and in 1967 an imaginative renovation programme was launched which resulted in its restoration to full working order. For details of opening times ring 01625 523012.

Nether Alderley Church

This is a fourteenth century building with a broad, low tower. Inside there is an unusual pew which resembles a box at a theatre. This is the Stanley

family pew decorated with the coats-of-arms of several important families to whom they are related. Their residence was Nether Alderley Hall which still stands on the opposite side of the A34.

The Route

From either of the two car parks turn right along London Road. By the major and complicated traffic junction opposite the Trafford Arms, make an acute left turn into Chapel Road, continuing along it as it becomes Mottram Road. Just beyond the cricket ground on your left swing right into "Squirrel's Jump".

This rough lane climbs for some 250 metres to a through stile which affords access to National Trust property. Stay with the broad track as it ascends for a further 100 metres before levelling out to contour the north face of the Edge.

After several hundred metres through magnificent beech and other deciduous trees a flight of wooden steps is reached. Turn right up these for a steep climb which arcs round to the left by several outcrops of red sandstone rock.

A short distance beyond where these terminate make a right turn up a shorter flight of steps and pass through two stone gateposts before making a left turn onto a large slab of rock which is known as "Castle Rock". This provides a panoramic view over the Cheshire Plain and Mersey Valley as far as the West Pennine Moors north of Bolton, recognised by the TV masts on Winter Hill. To the east the dominant peat plateaux of Kinder Scout and Bleaklow are two distinctive landmarks within the Peak District National Park.

From Castle Rock continue along the Edge, staying just to the left of a wire fence until reaching a stone wall on your right. By the corner of this turn right, taking any of the plethora of paths leading up to Beacon point, commemorated by a plaque set into a stone plinth.

Stay to the left of the Beacon, heading for a clear, well-maintained path identified by a wheelchair sign. At the next cross-roads in the path network continue straight ahead to the right of a very large patch of sandy ground running into a small valley.

This is where some of the former mines are located, so extreme care should be taken to avoid it. Maintain your direction along the path until emerging through a wooden stile onto a very broad path by the Wizard Tea Rooms and the National Trust Information Centre. Turn left, pass to the right of "Forester's Lodge" but, after 200 metres and just beyond a bend, make a right turn over a stile to walk between two wire fences.

Over the stile at the bottom of the dip climb to Edge House Farm, cross a broad track to another stile and lose height for a short distance down a field before turning right over another stile.

The path once again passes between wire fences but, after 50 metres and yet another stile, turns sharply to the left along a much broader track with a hedgerow on the left and a fence on the right.

At the foot of the gentle slope negotiate a stile but maintain your direction to the next stile where the waymarks offer a choice of three alternative routes.

Turn sharp right along the edge of a field and, after another stile, continue forward along a surfaced drive leading to Hill Top Farm which is a short distance off your route to the left.

100 metres beyond a cattle grid make a right turn over a stile to cross one field to Adders Moss Farm. Climb the stile alongside the garage, cross the driveway directly to another stile, walk just to the left of a hedge along the front of the house and turn right, as indicated by a waymarker arrow, before making a left turn over a stile.

Keep to the extreme right of a small paddock, climb a stile, continue forward to a large gate and pass a house on the left before reaching the B5087, the Alderley Edge to Macclesfield road.

Cross directly to the signed path running through Finlow Hill Wood. Where this short stretch ends turn right along a narrow surfaced road, passing a set of riding stables on your left. After a few hundred metres, follow the road round to the right but, where it swings right for a second time, continue directly ahead into Bradford Lane with its rough surface.

Stay with Bradford Lane to pass the Wizard Caravan Park until, a short distance beyond Bradford Lodge Farm, it acquires a cobbled surface.

By "The Spinney", Bradford Lane is joined from the left by Hocker Lane. Keep forward to reach the main road joining Manchester with Congleton, Birmingham and Southampton.

Turn left for the short distance to Alderley Mill which is on your left. 50 metres beyond this ancient monument make a right turn into the narrow road signed to Nether Alderley Church. Continue into the churchyard, passing to the right of the tiny school, constructed of local sandstone in 1628 at the expense of Hugh Shaw Clark, and the Mausoleum which houses the remains of former members of the Stanley family.

Keep to the left of the church itself to reach a gap in the facing wall. This has a small flight of steps leading down into the churchyard extension. Cross this to a kissing gate and maintain direction to a footpath plaque erected by the Peak and Northern Footpath Society alongside another gate. Pass throughthis and continue the same line across a large field following the footpath signed to Chorley.

Head for the gate in the facing hawthorn hedge. Cross directly over Sand Lane to a footpath finger post and keep to the footpath between a hedge to the left and fence to the right, flanked by houses on both sides.

After 100 metres pass beneath a giant oak and cross a wooden footbridge before veering very slightly to the left, as directed by the waymark, while aiming for a gap in the line of trees ahead.

Cross a footbridge and stay forward through an intermittent line of trees before heading for the left-hand corner of the boundary hedge surrounding a redbrick house. There, you will encounter a footpath sign alongside the field gate.

Exit onto Welsh Row, a narrow, surfaced road. Turn right for some 400 metres. Opposite Moseley House, turn left through a holly hedge onto a path as indicated by a footpath fingerpost.

The path keeps to the right of another hedge and to the left of a fence to a stile within 100 metres. Over this, continue between fences. On gaining the first field corner make a right turn over a stile and, with a wire fence on your left, walk along the field boundary until reaching a kissing gate, also on your left.

Turn left and, from this point onwards, the path develops into a lane lined on both sides by large trees. It crosses above the main Manchester to Crewe railway line by a bridge.

At the far end of the bridge, turn right over a stile as indicated by a fingerpost. and head diagonally across the field to a well-defined kink in the field boundary, marked also by the presence of a small pond. The railway moves further away to the right and the tall, conspicuous steeple of Alderley Edge Church visible in the far distance ahead. (Note: when last walked, this field had been sown with a crop and no track was visible. If you are not sure of the route, you may decide to follow the field edge instead to reach the same point.)

After reaching the boundary kink referred to above, cross the stile as instructed by a waymark, and continue to the left of the meandering field boundary. on the right. At the first footpath sign, cross a footbridge and stile on the right and continue to a stile alongside a gate. Cross the stile onto a wide track and pass over the railway again.

Soon, pass houses with brick garden walls on your left and join a tarmac road. This leads through a small housing development to a T junction. Turn right here to the De Trafford Arms on the main road, where you turn left and return to your starting point.

Walk 18: Prestbury

Route	Prestbury - Spittle House - Woodend Farm - Legh hall - Mottram Wood - Bollin Valley - Prestbury
Start	New Road, Prestbury, near the Legh Arms. Map reference SJ900769
Distance	4 miles
Map	OS Explorer 268, Wilmslow, Macclesfield & Congleton
Getting there by public transport	Prestbury station is served by frequent daily (including Sunday) trains from Manchester, Stockport, Macclesfield and Stoke-on-Trent. Prestbury is also served by frequent buses from Macclesfield and Wilmslow (Monday to Friday)
Getting there by car	Prestbury is about three miles north of Macclesfield and may be reached by either of two minor roads from the A523 or the A538 from Wilmslow. There are two large, free car parks in the village

The Tea Shops

The Bridge Hotel

Once a row of timbered cottages, one of which provided lodging for Bonnie Prince Charlie as he travelled south with his Scottish army in 1745, the buildings were acquired in 1952 and developed into the hotel and restaurant that we see today. With your morning coffee or afternoon tea, choose from pastries, scones, flapjacks and other goodies. Normally served in the hotel lounge but also in the terraced courtyard and garden in the summer. Lunches are available in the restaurant.

The Bridge Hotel

Opening hours: normal hotel hours, every day of the week, all year. Tel: 01625 829326.

The Chocolate Box

The original Chocolate Box closed a few years ago. Fortunately, its successor reopened in October 2011 just next door in the capable hands of Angela O'Leary (pictured to the right) and Katharine Nuttall.

The Chocolate Box

Completely refurbished and attractively decorated, walkers will find a good range of cakes and light lunches. For a special treat, champagne breakfasts are offered from Friday to Sunday, with the tinkling of a piano providing extra elegance. Traditional afternoon teas are also available, with savoury and children's options.

Opening hours: Monday to Friday 8am to 6pm . Tel: 01625 827876.

Prestbury

The name "Prestbury" is derived from "Priests' Burgh" and is indicative of a very early Christian foundation with a group of clergy serving a very wide area. As proof of this there is a fragment of an Anglo-Saxon stone cross, discovered during the nineteenth century and now preserved in a glass case in the churchyard.

Also in the churchyard is a Norman chapel which was rebuilt during the eighteenth century. Much of the present church dates from the thirteenth century with later additions and alterations and includes memorials to several local families.

Another reminder of Prestbury's medieval history is the Spittle House. Today it is a private residence but originally, as its name implies, it was a hospital run by the church authorities.

The village itself is a mixture of architectural styles from medieval black and white half-timbered houses through Georgian to nineteenth century weavers' cottages. The Priest's House, built in 1448, remains in use as a bank and the large white house at the southern end of the main street is Prestbury Hall.

Walk 18 Prestbury

The Route

From the start point close to the junction of Macclesfield Road and Wilmslow Road in the centre of Prestbury, turn right along New Road, to pass Prestbury church.

Cross the stone bridge over the River Bollin, here flowing over a cobbled bed, and turn left into Bollin Grove which is signed as part of the Bollin Way to Wilmslow.

The Bollin Valley Way runs for 30 miles from the Macclesfield Riverside Park to the Manchester Ship Canal along the banks of the River Bollin. It was established under the auspices of the Bollin Valley Project, an experimental pilot scheme launched by the Countryside Commission in 1973 to develop open-air recreation in the countryside along the urban fringes.

The river is now on your left but look out for the colourful garden of "Riverside Cottage" on your right, a short distance before passing the Methodist Church.

Bollin Grove continues beyond the village school and a row of old redbrick cottages intermingled with more substantial modern residences. Where Bollin Grove ends, with a playing field on your left and another Bollin Valley way sign on your right, maintain direction along a broad chatter track.

On approaching a concrete bridge with white railings, ignore a stile on your right and yet another sign pointing towards Wilmslow. Instead, go left over the Bollin with the track. A short distance in front of Spittle House, go left over a stile to follow a field path as it runs to the left of a hedge of copper beech to another stile.

Continue close to the hedge and then, in the far corner of the field, turn right over a stile, advancing about 30 metres to a waymarker post. There, turn left down a flight of steps, climb another stile, negotiate a footbridge over the stream and climb five wooden steps. At the head of these swing left, aiming for a stile in the corner of the field.

Over that advance a further 10 metres to a second stile and then walk a little to the right of a wire fence. Half way along the field boundary and by a metal gate, turn left over a stile to pass a small coppice of trees planted by the Bollin Valley Project.

Keeping the fence on your right, continue to the corner of the field before reaching a stile on the right which provides access to a broad lane. Turn left along this but, where it ends, cross the driveway leading to Woodend Farm, climb the obvious stile and follow the path signed to Mottram St Andrew as it crosses the field.

Stay forward to a solitary chestnut tree, lose altitude slightly to a wooden footbridge over a marshy area and maintain the same line of direction towards the right-hand corner of another coppice.

Advance with this on your left but, by the far corner, swing sharply to the left and head for a waymarker post while staying to the right of a line of hawthorn trees. Over the next stile continue with a ditch and fence on your left, ignoring a sign showing a path off to the left towards Prestbury Road.

Negotiate another stile and partner the hedge on your left while proceeding round the corner of the field to another footpath sign. Directed by this, turn left through a metal kissing gate onto a broad track, soon reaching a junction in the network of lanes by Legh Hall.

Turn right by the footpath signpost, walking by the side of Legh Hall itself to another kissing gate. Through this, traverse the long meadow in a straight line, climb a stile on the left and, maintaining the same general line of direction, keep forward to Woodside Farm.

Cross the driveway directly, negotiate a stile and then turn sharp right to pass alongside the barn and a spasmodic row of trees to another stile which provides access to Mottram Wood.

The path through this is clear and easy to follow until it emerges into a large grass paddock surrounded on all sides by mature deciduous trees. This spot is rural Cheshire at its finest.

Cross the paddock in a straight line, climb a stile, turn right as directed by a footpath sign and descend to a footbridge spanning the River Bollin. On the far bank turn right along the riverside path, staying with it beyond the Water Treatment Works until it emerges onto Bollin Grove. Retrace your steps to the start point.

Walk 19: Bollington

Route	Bollington - Oakenbank - Rainow - Kerridge Hill - Lower Swanscoe - Swanscoe - Macclesfield Canal - Bollington
Start	Pool Bank car park, Palmerston Street, Bollington. Map reference SJ937779
Distance	6 miles (short option: 3 miles)
Map	OS Explorer 268, Wilmslow, Macclesfield & Congleton
Getting there by public transport	Frequent daily buses between Bollington and Macclesfield, from where there are excellent rail and bus connections
Getting there by car	From the main A523 Macclesfield to Hazel Grove road, take the B5090 or B5091 through Bollington. Pass under the viaduct and then the aqueduct and you soon see Pool Bank car park on the left, almost opposite to High Street. If full, park considerately in a nearby street

Earlier editions featured a walk around Kettleshulme but, as there is no longer a café in the area, nearby Bollington is featured instead. This walk is based on one in "East Cheshire Walks" by Graham Beech, also from Sigma Leisure, but suitably amended to include a tea shop!

The Tea Shop

You might imagine that, given the range of walks radiating from the village, there would be a wide choice of tea shops in Bollington. Surprisingly, there are very few, but here is a real gem: Café Waterside in the Clarence Mill building alongside the canal. There's plenty of seating inside and on sunny days (which do happen!) it's pleasant to sit outside to watch the world – and the narrow boats – go by.

Catering, overseen by Julie Taylor, is of a very high standard with a tempting display of cakes and scones for morning coffee or afternoon tea. Call in at lunchtime and the range is even wider with piping-hot homemade soup, salads, rolls and a choice of hot dishes.

Café Waterside in the Clarence Mill building alongside the canal

Opening hours: Tuesday to Sunday, 10.15am to 5.00pm. Closed Mondays but open most Bank Holidays. Tel: 01625-575563.

Monday alternatives: a basic option is The Bridgend Centre (community cooperative), 104 Palmerston Street; Open Monday – Thursday, 10.00am – 4.30pm, Saturday 10.00am – 3.00pm. 01625 576311. More up-market: the Maggoty Johnson Café Bar and Restaurant, High Street; open daily 11.30am through to 10.30 or 11.00pm; 01625-574699.

Bollington

The village is now mainly residential, with many of the old terraced houses providing ideal first homes. Not so long ago, however, it was a hive of industry with quarrying, mining, and up to 20 mills connected with the cotton, flour and paper industries – and about the same number of pubs where the workers could slake their thirsts. There's still the canal, but the railway closed in 1971 – imagine how popular it would be now as a commuter line! Instead, it has been adapted as a linear route for walkers, cyclists and horse riders.

Bollington offers its residents a very active social life – see **www.happy-valley.org.uk** for an overview of what's happening. Attractions include the

Bollington Festival every four years or so (**www.bollingtonfestival.org.uk**), an Arts Centre in the middle of the village, the Discovery Centre in Clarence Mill and Canalside Community radio station (**www.ccr-fm.co.uk**).

The Route

Turn left out of the car park and walk uphill, passing "The Plaice" and some traditional local shops. At the bus turning area, fork right to pass the New Con club and continue uphill along Ingersley Road. Turn right at the Poachers Inn, then along Mill Lane (2). This narrows to a stony track and you soon keep left past a small row of cottages. Just at the back of the very last cottage, and before a factory, turn left to climb stone steps (4), then follow the path uphill. This soon bears right and levels out, with a gritstone wall on your left.

Look out for a combination of steps and a stile in the wall. Cross the stile (4), turn right and, after about 30m, turn left onto a wide grassy track leading slightly uphill towards a gates and a stile.

Cross the main drive to Savio House. Until the 1970s, this was Ingersley Hall Farm, but is now a retreat and conference centre run by the Salesian religious order. Continue along a wide, raised track towards a small wood (keep it on your left) then go through a kissing gate to a stony track (5). Turn immediately right after a step stile and right again to cross a stile with a Gritstone Trail marker, then walk downhill, with a wall on your right. Long ago, this path was used by the men and women who walked to Bollington every day to work in the mills. It still has much of the original stone steps and paving.

Climb uphill to pass a white-painted house. After two stiles, you will find a third stile almost immediately on your right. Cross this but then turn left and continue on the right of the wall in roughly the same direction as before – i.e. do not walk downhill. On your right, as you pass through this field, you will see the White Nancy monument at one end of Kerridge Hill.

Continue to the end of the field. Go over the stile that's facing you and walk straight ahead to cross a stile in the far-left corner. After entering this next field, cross a stile half-way along the opposite wall. The next stile is in the far-right-hand corner – squeeze through this and turn left towards Rainow, passing through two more stiles and down a stone-slabbed slope. Soon, on your right, you will see the lake and gardens of Hough Hole House, complete with its Victorian Allegorical Garden and stone plaques along a path representing the story of 'A Pilgrim's Progress'. The gardens are currently open on the late May Bank Holiday and August

Walk 19 Bollington

N

River Dean

B5091

To
Prestbury

Bollington

White Nancy
(monument)

Kerridge

Kerridge Hill

Rainow

To
Horwich End

Moat Hall
Farm

Macclesfield Canal

B5470

Brookhouse

Swanscoe
Hall

B5470

To
Macclesfield

0   500m

Bank Holiday Mondays and to groups by prior arrangement at other times – phone 01625 573251 for details.

You soon reach a minor road. Turn right here (6). After 100m, turn left up some steps (7) into a field. Keep to the right and head downhill, then cross a stile and two footbridges over streams. From here, head steeply uphill, roughly parallel to power cables on your right, towards a gap in the trees at the top of Kerridge Hill (8).

Carry on over the top of the hill, then turn left alongside a wall and head steeply downhill to a road. Cross the road and turn right (9) along the wide track to Endon House. After almost 300m, and before any of the buildings, take a sharp left hairpin alongside a wide steel gate (10). After a few minutes, cross a stile beside a wide wooden gate. Soon after, turn left through a gate with yellow waymarks. Follow the path straight ahead and pass through a gate to join the drive for Swanscoe Farm.

From here, ignore your OS map – the rights of way were diverted in 2009. This is the the revised route: ignore the gate facing you across the tarmac drive; instead, turn left up the drive. Ignore the next gate on your right but, in another 20m or so, turn right through a gate with waymarks. Go down a flight of steps and turn left to follow the waymarks – there is a large ornamental pond below and to your right. The right of way soon emerges onto the drive to Lower Swanscoe Farm, where you turn left and continue for half a mile to a road.

Turn right here and, keeping to the right along Swanscoe Lane, pass the entrance to Swanscoe Hall (11). After 200m or so, bear right down a road signed as a 'dead end' and, after about 100m, enter the private drive (12) signed to 'Woodlands, Woodend and Shrigley Fold'. After the second property, fork right on a signed footpath. Pass buildings on your left and follow the waymarks gently downhill, soon following a farm track towards a ruined barn. Just before the barn, turn left and pass to the right of an old mine shaft, now filled in. Go straight ahead from here on an obvious track to a small pool by a kissing gate. Go through this and, with the hedge on your left, follow the waymarks to cross the next stile and pass between two pools to yet another opposite stile.

Along the way, you may notice numbered plaques on stiles and other locations. These relate to "Nostalgia Trails" developed by the Bridgend Centre. For more information on the centre and the trails, visit **http://tinyurl.com/cpt8kv**

Cross a track, another stile, and bear right to follow the path to the left of yet another pool – they like pools around here – and continue to the road (13), where you turn left towards the canal. Cross the bridge over the canal and turn right down the steps to the towpath. It's now an easy stroll to the centre of Bollington, first passing the Adelphi Mill and then heading onwards to Clarence Mill, marked by its tall brick chimney.

Cross the canal at bridge 26a, which was opened in 2009 after a lengthy campaign supported by local residents. Turn left to walk a short distance between the mill and the canal, to your destination: Café Waterside. If it has been a muddy walk, note that there is usually a supply of boot bags. After a scrumptious break, turn left from the café then head downhill to traffic lights. Turn left here and stroll back to your car.

Walk 20: Wildboarclough

Route	Blaze Farm - Wildboarclough - Three Shire Heads - Cumberland Clough - Wildboarclough - Blaze Farm
Start	Blaze Farm, near Allgreave. Map reference SJ974676
Distance	7¼ miles
Map	OS Outdoor Leisure Series No. 24, The Peak District; White Peak Area
Getting there by public transport	Restricted bus service from Macclesfield
Getting there by car	Blaze Farm is near Allgreave, on the A54, Buxton to Congleton road

The Tea Shop

Blaze Farm is on a hillside above Wildboarclough. It's still very much a working farm, but is also renowned for its Hilly Billy ice-cream. You can tuck into this in the excellent café based on two adapted milking parlours – the smaller one described as "relaxing" and a larger one that's ideal for families. With your morning coffee or afternoon tea, enjoy home-made cakes, scones or apple pie (with ice-cream, of course!). At lunchtime, choose from sandwiches, Staffordshire oatcakes, jacket potatoes and ploughman's platters. In the winter, beef hotpot is usually on the menu. It's a family-friendly place where children can feed the hens and ducks, see lambs in the springtime and sheep-shearing in the summer, and watch the cows being milked. There is also a nature trail for older children to learn about the countryside.

Opening hours: 10am to 5pm, Tuesday to Sunday, all year.

Note: Walkers should park in the overflow car park and are expected to patronise the café or to purchase from the shop in lieu of a charge for parking!

Wildboarclough

Regarded by many people as one of the most attractive valleys in the Peak District National Park, Wildboarclough lies entirely within the county of

Cheshire. Although popular with visitors at week-ends, the crowds are soon left behind by those walking the abundance of footpaths radiating out from this dramatic moorland valley.

Though it is tempting to associate its name with wild boars, its origin is said to be more prosaic, being a corruption of "valley of the wild stream". Though now predominantly agricultural, the area has been exploited for small-scale quarrying and was mined for coal until the early 20th century. There is some evidence for charcoal production, the "Blaze" in "Blaze Hill" being a strong clue. The valley was home to three water-powered silk mills during the eighteenth century when the canal pioneer, James Brindley, installed some of the machinery. In later years the mills turned to the production of carpets, some of which were featured in the Great Exhibition of 1851. Most of the mills have been demolished, though the old Post Office and the present Youth Hostel at Gradbach are reminders of some grand old buildings. Much of the land in the area is owned by the Earl of Derby who used Crag Hall as one of his country seats.

In 1989, a freak thunderstorm and cloud-burst over the moorlands surrounding the "Cat and Fiddle" at the head of the valley created a flash flood which rushed down the bed of Clough Brook and tributary streams. One person died: roads, bridges, cars, trees and drystone walls were swept away. Many footpaths were obliterated.

A quick response by Cheshire County Council, aided by the Countryside Commission, Macclesfield Borough Council, the Peak District National Park and other bodies resulted in speedy restoration, albeit at enormous cost. One benefit has been the renewal of footbridges, footpaths and footpath signs.

The Route

Walk from the tea room towards the farm drive, then turn right down a tarmac track signed to the Nature Pond. Walk between the two ponds, cross the cow track and go left down a concrete track, this being a concessionary path. Turn right at the bottom of the track, now on a public right of way. Follow the waymarked route, soon with Clough Brook on the left. After a 10-minute stroll, turn left across a bridge then right at the road. As you walk along this road, catch glimpses, on your left, of Shutlingsloe – the "Matterhorn of Cheshire",

Just past the Crag Inn, turn right at a signpost and cross the river. Walk uphill, wall on right and stream on left, cross a stile at the top end of a wood and continue uphill towards a wall corner. Here, bear right over a

Three Shire Heads

footbridge and cross another footbridge soon afterwards. Turn left at a signpost below woodland protected by a wall and head for the buildings of Firs Farm. Go through a gateway then straight ahead on a farm track which eventually leads to a road junction.

Turn right here, uphill, for a few minutes and then fork left (signpost to Three Shire Heads) along a wide stone-wall-lined track. You're soon on a grassy track that leads over the hillside to the A54. Cross this busy road and follow a well-used path, at first straight ahead but soon bearing left after a footbridge. Continue to a stile with two waymarks and follow the one that forks left. Carry on towards a building, after which you cross a stile onto a country lane. Turn right here and then, after just a few metres, left onto a stony track. (Note: no dogs allowed along here, but dog owners can avoid this restriction by continuing downhill to Knar, then swinging north-east on a parallel track in the valley – see OS map). Either of these routes leads you to Three Shire Heads – the place where the counties of Cheshire, Staffordshire and Derbyshire meet. It's a picturesque spot and just about half-way round, so an ideal place to take a break.

Walk 20 Wildboarclough

N

Whetstone Ridge

To Buxton

Shutlingsloe

Mount Pleasant

Wildboarclough

Cut-thorn Hill

A54

Blaze Farm

Birchenough Hill

A54

To Congleton

Midgley Hill

River Dane

Gradbach Hill

0   1km

To continue the walk, do not cross the bridge, but continue on the track with the river to your right. After passing through a gateway, the track starts to climb and soon there's a waymark pointing even further uphill, with a large farm over to your right. Pass through a gateway and bear left before the next gate. Follow the wall towards the left-hand of two large ladder stiles and climb steeply towards this stile. Cross it and continue across the A54 (again!) to a wide, stony track with a "No cars allowed, except for access" sign.

This is a splendid route with wonderful views. Continue to the head of Cumberland Clough, a deep gorge marked by a considerable waterfall – a photogenic spot. Turn left after the waterfall (signpost to Wildboarclough) and walk down the clough, eventually crossing Cumberland Brook and joining a minor road. Cross here to Clough House Farm, go through the farmyard and follow the waymark over Clough Brook. Cross the road and join the footpath (signed to Langley – a pleasant route that avoids the road}. After about 10 minutes, you pass a house and are soon walking down a tarmac drive to the road.

Turn right at the road, pass the Crag Inn and all will soon start to look familiar, as you are now re-tracing your outward route. So, carry on past the Brookside parking area, then turn left at the postbox, cross the bridge and immediately turn right. Follow the waymarks, initially with the river on your right and just keep walking. Pass two houses and then, 150 metres after the YHA camping barn, turn left up the signed concessionary path that seems to be steeper than it was at the start of the walk!

In a very short time, you're back at Blaze Farm, nicely in time for tea. Or whatever.

Walk 21: Lyme Park

Route	Lyme Hall - Crow Wood - Elmerhurst Cottage - Cockhead Farm - Bollinhurst Bridge - East Lodge - Lyme Hall
Start	The main car park, Lyme Park, Disley. Map reference SJ963824. An alternative start may be made from the main entrance on the A6
Distance	4½ miles
Map	OS Outdoor Leisure Series No. 1, The Peak District; Dark Peak Area
Getting there by public transport	The main entrance to Lyme Park on the A6 north of Disley is served by frequent daily (including Sunday) buses from Manchester, Stockport, Buxton, Bakewell, Matlock, Derby and Nottingham. There are frequent daily (including Sunday) trains from Manchester, Stockport and Buxton to Disley station, about half a mile from the main entrance
Getting there by car	The main entrance to Lyme Park is on the A6, a few miles south of Stockport and about half a mile north of Disley. The main car park is approximately one mile inside the park from the entrance. Entrance fee

The Tea Shops

The former Lakeside Café, is now known as the Timber Yard Coffee shop. It is located in the same building, a large, airy brick affair overlooking the lake close to the car park. The interior has white painted walls, wooden block floors and large wooden roof beams.

The menu, which is extensive, includes soup of the day with roll, salads and home-made cakes that vary daily but usually include such favourites as flapjack, carrot cake, Victoria Sponge and chocolate fudge. There is a separate children's menu. All may be accompanied by a choice of speciality teas and coffees or soft drinks.

Opening hours: 11am to 4pm, open all year. Tel: 01663 762023.

For a quick break, there is also a kiosk by the main car park; seasonal opening.

Lyme Hall

The home of the Legh family for more than 600 years, Lyme Hall contains interiors from various periods of history including Elizabethan, Stuart, Georgian and Edwardian. The present house is a splendid example of eighteenth century Palladian architecture by the Italian Giacomo Leoni which was altered a century later by Lewis Wyatt. The contents include furniture from various periods, numerous family portraits and an outstanding collection of English clocks.

Mary Queen of Scots visited Lyme while staying at Buxton as a prisoner of Queen Elizabeth I and guarded by the Earl of Shrewsbury.

The gardens extend over more than 16 acres and include formal parterres, herbaceous borders, a Victorian conservatory and an Edwardian rose garden. The setting is a vast moorland park of 1,300 acres which is home to herds of red and fallow deer.

Lyme Cage is the square tower some distance from the hall. Built as an observation tower for watching the progress of the hunt, it was later used as a lock-up for poachers.

Lyme Hall

The Route

Exit the car park by the kiosk and make a left turn along the surfaced drive, passing to the left of the small lake. Follow this drive around the exterior of the car park as it swings round to the right for a very short climb. At the top of the rise fork right onto an unsurfaced track at the first Y-junction. After a further 120 metres, and by a wall corner, a second Y-junction is reached.

Fork right again, advancing along another rough track which accompanies a stone wall on your right while directly ahead is a wide view over Greater Manchester. As the track begins to lose height, negotiate a stile adjacent to two gates and stay forward but, 15 metres beyond, turn right over a ladder stile to take the path alongside the drystone wall forming the field boundary.

The reward at this stage is a view of the western fringes of the Peak District hills of Bleaklow and Kinder Scout. Below, but closer to hand on the left, is Platt Wood Farm.

Negotiate a wooden stile alongside a gate and, on the immediate right, a stone field barn with a rusty corrugated metal roof. Continue close to the wall and over a stone step stile in the field corner to advance to the left of Crow Wood.

Descend briefly but somewhat steeply onto a wide track that forms the approach to Platt Wood Farm, now but a short distance to your left. Cross directly to the left of the cattle grid and proceed through a metal gate before following the path over a large field.

Veer gradually away from the wall on your left as you climb, initially aiming for a clump of trees. However, on the crown of the rise, swing leftwards to pass about midway between the trees, now on your right, and the wall on your left.

Make a line towards a clearly visible gate in the distant fence ahead. On reaching this you will find a stile some 15 metres to the right. Negotiate this before striking out over the next field while aiming for the far right-hand corner. The path, having passed between an oak tree on the left and a zinc water trough on the right, eventually meets a wide track in front of a facing drystone wall.

Turn right and pass to the left of "Elmerhurst Cottage" before negotiating a very small wooden gate followed, within 20 metres, by a large white metal one. Continue over two small bridges and by "Brookside Cottages" before meeting the main driveway into the park, a few metres to the right of the entrance from the A6.

Cross the drive to the left of the wooden kiosk but, by the first corner of "Red Lane Cottage", turn left through a tall wooden gate onto a lane which passes to the right of some boarding kennels and the complex belonging to the United Utilities plc.

Leaving these behind continue along the lane. Ignore a footpath signed off to the left after 350 metres, climbing more steeply for a further 100 metres.

By the first corner of the first house and by another footpath sign, turn right over a wooden stile. Keep to the right of a stone wall with a lapwood fence on top and parallel with some overhead wires.

Over the stile in the field corner, turn left through ninety degrees to pass to the right of a private tennis court and a row of holly and hawthorn trees until arriving at the surfaced approach lane to Bollinhurst Reservoir. Turn right along this for a quarter of a mile. By the derelict Cockhead Farm and before a set of double wooden gates turn left to negotiate an unsigned stile adjacent to a metal gate.

Do not go through these wooden gates because the path beyond leads to the reservoir enclosure which is forbidden to the public. Instead, remain to the left of a wire fence until the first field corner. There swing left to a rather large telegraph pole before veering to the right and staying to the left of a drystone wall. This wall separates you from Bollinhurst Reservoir while Horse Coppice Reservoir is behind you.

Over a stone step stile in the next wall corner continue alongside the wall until, beyond the head of Bollinhurst Reservoir, the path swings left to enter some woods by a strange and unusual stile which has three uprights.

Having negotiated this, swing slightly to the left, traverse a low ridge between two streams and emerge into a very green pasture. Follow the clear path across the greensward until it reaches a bridleway by a Peak and Northern Footpath Society sign adjacent to a stile.

Ignore a facing path signed to Kettleshulme and turn right along the sunken lane which is lined with oak, holly, sycamore and bramble, not to mention foxglove. Lose height before crossing Bollinhurst Bridge and climbing steeply to re-enter Lyme Park by the gate at East Lodge.

The track traverses high ground so affording some views of the surrounding moorlands. Lyme Cage eventually appears to your right with red deer grazing all around it. The going is easy and relaxed. Continue until the track acquires a surface and loses height to pass in front of Lyme Hall. If you desire the Tea Rooms turn left through the Hall entrance. Otherwise, continue forward down a long flight of steps leading to both the Coffee Shop and the car park.

Walk 22: Pott Shrigley

Route	Coffee Tavern - Moorside Lane - Keeper's Cottage - Sponds Hill - Bowstonegate - Knightslow Wood - Coffee Tavern
Start	The Coffee Tavern near Pott Shrigley. Map reference SJ944803
Distance	5 miles
Map	OS Explorer 268, Wilmslow, Macclesfield & Congleton
Getting there by public transport	None
Getting there by car	The Coffee Tavern is situated on the minor road from Pott Shrigley to Higher Poynton and is signed from Norman's Hall Farm (map reference SJ936801). Ask permission before leaving your car in the car park. There are very few safe places to park on the road

The Tea Shop

Unusually the Coffee Tavern is constructed of corrugated metal sheeting. It was built in 1897 as a Public Reading Room and Library by Miss Eleanor Constance Lowther, a member of the local landed family, to mark the Diamond Jubilee of Queen Victoria. It was also used for church services and for social gatherings for the local inhabitants. After ceasing to fulfil its original function between the two World Wars it was converted to the Coffee Tavern and Tea Rooms.

In those days it was extremely popular with ramblers from the Manchester and Stockport areas. After the Second World War trade declined and it was converted into a storage depot by a local plumber. It was eventually re-opened as the Coffee Tavern by its owner at the suggestion of his son, Andrew Buffey, a trained chef who is now in charge of all the cooking.

It serves snacks and full meals throughout the day and is renowned for its home-baked scones, cream gateaux, cakes and other delicacies, one of

Walk 22 Pott Shrigley

To Higher Poynton

Macclesfield Canal

N

Lyme Hall

Knightslow Wood

Park Moor

Gritstone Trail

Unwin Pool

Coffee Tavern
Birchencliff

Keeper's Cottage

Sponds Hill

Bakestonedale Moor

Pott Shrigley

Brink Brow

To Horwich End

B5470

Harrop Brook

To Bollington

0   500m

To Macclesfield

the most popular dishes being Sticky Toffee Pudding. These are all washed down with an admirable choice of coffees or speciality teas served in generous pots.

Opening hours: Closed on Tuesdays and on Christmas Day, otherwise open all year from 10.00am to 6.00pm except for a two-week break some time in February – so check first. Tel: 01625 576370.

The Route

Leaving the Coffee Tavern, turn left along the road in the direction of Pott Shrigley. After a very short distance turn left again, leaving the surfaced road for a bridleway which climbs steadily towards Birchencliff Farm, a pleasant dwelling surrounded by trees.

Negotiate the stone stile alongside the small pool which belongs to Ryder Brow Fishing Club and continue along the bridleway which, after a short respite, resumes its gradual climb through a landscape of shallow valleys and green, rounded hills.

Beyond the next gate proceed for 10 metres before turning left into Moorside Lane, another bridleway. After 300 metres, and just before "Keeper's Cottage", turn right onto a footpath signed to Kettleshulme and Bowstones. This continues upwards to the right of a partially collapsed drystone wall until it reaches a makeshift gate between the end of a fence and a wall on Planted Moor.

Keep to the same line for 100 metres until the path is joined by another coming in from the right. From this junction maintain direction along the edge of Bakestonedale Moor as the wide path undulates for approximately one mile.

Over the wall on your left is the upper moor of Lyme Park where a large herd of red deer is often to be seen at close hand. To the right there is an extensive panorama towards the Cheshire Plain and the Triangulation Pillar on Sponds Hill confirms that you have reached a height of 410 metres above sea level.

After passing to the left of a small brick wall with concrete culverts set into it, negotiate another gate before crossing about 150 metres of boggy ground to meet a bridleway. This traverses the high moors from Brink Farm on the Pott Shrigley to Whaley Bridge road to Bowstonegate and forms part of the Gritstone Trail.

Turn left along this until negotiating a gate by Bowstones Farm. This stretch of the route offers some splendid views out over the Goyt Valley to Kinder Scout and South Head. Through the gate, and where the rough surface ends, turn left over a stile. With the Bowstones and Bowstones

Farm on your right, advance to a second stile.

Stay with the well-worn path as it descends the rough moorland until meeting a ladder stile alongside a gate at the entrance to Knightslow Wood. Do not negotiate the stile. Turn left along another broad track which dips slightly to cross a stream before climbing a little and then traversing a level stretch of moorland for a considerable distance until reaching a stile.

Over this the path develops into a wide track, Moorside Lane. Proceed beyond Moorside Farm, a short distance to your right, until reaching "Keeper's Cottage". From there retrace your outward steps to the Coffee Tavern.

The Coffee Tavern

Walk 23: Poynton

Route	Higher Poynton - Haresteads Farm - Throstle Nest - Green Farm - Lockgate Farm - Macclesfield Canal - Poynton Coppice - Higher Poynton
Start	Nelson Pit Visitor Centre, Lyme Road, Higher Poynton. Map reference SJ940835
Distance	4½ miles
Map	OS Explorer 268, Wilmslow, Macclesfield & Congleton
Getting there by public transport	The start is served by frequent daily (including Sunday) buses from Manchester and Stockport
Getting there by car	The start may be reached by a minor road from the A523 in the centre of Poynton village or from Pott Shrigley, turning right at Norman's Hall Farm. The car park is by the Visitor Centre, just a short distance along the road opposite to the Boar's Head

The Tea Shops

Our main choice is the Original Coffee Tavern next door to the nearby Boar's Head. Scones, cakes, muffins and snacks, sandwiches & barms are available with the opportunity to dine in the garden if the weather is good. Closed on Mondays.

The Trading Post (by the canal, just minutes before the end of the walk) has DIY tea and coffee, packets of biscuits and chocolate bars. Some outside seating. Closed on Wednesdays.

Nelson Pit Visitor Centre

Don't just dash out of the car park to start your walk: call in at the Visitor Centre to learn about the area in general, and Poynton in particular. Both young and old will enjoy finding out about the past, thanks to the well-designed displays. There is an excellent selection of leaflets about nearby attractions. Note also that there are toilets here.

The Macclesfield Canal

This canal forms a link between the Peak Forest Canal at Marple in Greater Manchester, and the Trent and Mersey Canal at Kidsgrove in Staffordshire, a distance of 26 miles.

It shares with the Peak Forest Canal the distinction of being the highest navigable waterway in England. It passes over the nearby town of Bollington by means of a spectacular aqueduct and at Bosley, to the south of Macclesfield, there is an impressive flight of 12 locks.

In its heyday it transported stone from nearby quarries, coal from the mines at Poynton and textiles from Macclesfield and Bollington. The Macclesfield Canal is reputed to have formed the cornerstone of Pickfords' transport business. The canal eventually declined with the opening of a railway line between Macclesfield and Marple. In recent years the towpath has been improved by British Waterways and Macclesfield Borough Council for use by walkers.

The Middlewood Way

This special walking route was opened by Stockport Metropolitan Borough Council and Macclesfield Borough Council in 1985. It runs along the track of the former railway line which linked Macclesfield with Rose Hill, Marple.

It is about 11 miles long and has many access points. Horse riding and cycling are also permitted and there is a cycle hire centre operated by the Macclesfield Groundwork Trust in Bollington.

Poynton

During the eighteenth and nineteenth centuries Poynton was the centre of a thriving coal mining industry with several small mines on or near the canal and railway. In later years it became noted for the quality of the bricks manufactured there. Now it is mainly residential.

The Route

Turn left from the Visitor Centre car park onto the road and walk uphill, soon crossing the canal bridge. Stay forward along the rough track to reach a cattle grid by a white house on your left. A short distance beyond this a Y-junction is reached. Take the right-hand track to maintain direction, originally staying close to the wood on your right where the silver birch are festooned with small bracket fungus.

Negotiate a small wicket gate to the right of another cattle grid and pass through open pastoral countryside before embarking on a gentle descent

Walk 23 Poynton

Higher Poynton

Macclesfield Canal

Platt Wood

S

Café

Café

Haresteads

Poynton Brook

Throstle Nest Farm

Green Farm

Middlewood Way

Wood Lanes

Macclesfield Canal

Redacre Hall Farm

Lock Gate

0   500m

N

to a gate alongside a third cattle grid where a culverted stream is crossed. From this point the track begins a gentle climb to Haresteads Farm. By the first corner of the farmhouse turn right into the farmyard and then immediately make another right turn to a wicket gate. Through that, turn sharply to the left, walking alongside a corrugated metal building on your left. Where that ends continue forward to the right of a wire fence and down a very short stretch of rough pasture to a wooden stile. Over this there follows a very short climb through a clump of trees to the skeleton of a disintegrating wooden hut already swamped by vegetation.

By this turn right to reach a stile after 75 metres. Continue to the left of a hedge until passing through a gate a few metres before Throstle Nest Farm. Swing right to a small waymarked gate after a few metres and then follow the signs around the outside of the buildings and garden, on your left, until emerging into a small field by means of a stile.

Turn left, still to the right of the farm and, with a hedge on your left, round the first field corner. In the second corner negotiate a stile, turn left again and, still staying close to that hedge on your left, advance a further 20 metres to another stile which provides access to a wide track. This tortuous navigation avoids a straightforward but forbidden route through the farmyard.

Turn right along the track, climbing to Green Farm. By the first corner of the farmhouse turn right to join a broad track which is signed a few metres beyond the house. By a small pond on your right, this track twists through a Z-bend and over a cattle grid before straightening to continue its course to another cattle grid and descending to pass to the right of West Park Gate Farm.

Cross a stone bridge and ignore a signed path to the right. Remain with the track until it emerges onto the Pott Shrigley road by Green Close Methodist Church. Turn left, climbing for approximately 100 metres until the road levels. After a similar distance and a few metres before a white house, turn right by a footpath sign into Simpson's Lane which descends by a cottage which takes its name from the bridleway.

Continue beyond this cottage but a short distance before reaching the impressive buildings of Redacres Hall Farm, and by a telegraph pole, turn left over a stile which has "To Lockgate Farm" painted on it in white letters.

The clear, unmistakable path worms its way across the field, heading for the left-hand corner of Lockgate Farm. There, turn right over a stile, and staying to the right of the farm buildings, advance to a second waymarked stile which is followed by a lane.

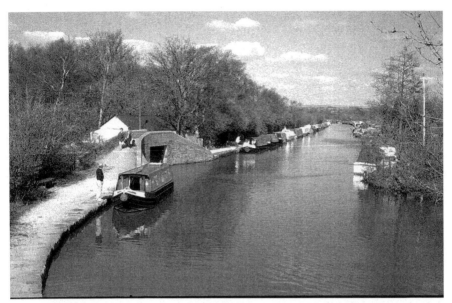

Adlington Basin

Continue along this for more than a quarter of a mile until it crosses over the Macclesfield Canal by a hump-backed bridge by Woods Lane Marina (Adlington Basin).

You now have a choice of route. Canal lovers can turn right along the towpath of the Macclesfield Canal and return to the starting point, passing "The Trading Post" along the way.

The alternative is to continue for a few yards and turn right along the Middlewood Way. Eventually this will lead you through the car park at Poynton Coppice and then to the site of the former railway station at Higher Poynton. This is now a picnic site and is opposite to the Boar's Head and the "Original Coffee Tavern".

Walk 24: Styal

Route	Quarry Bank Mill - Norcliffe Chapel - Willow Cottage - Golf Course - Clay Lane - Linney's Bridge - Quarry Bank Mill
Start	The car park, Quarry Bank Mill and Styal Country Park. Map reference SJ835831. Or Styal village if using the alternative tea room (see below)
Distance	3½ miles
Map	OS Explorer 268, Wilmslow, Macclesfield & Congleton
Getting there by public transport	Styal is served by frequent daily buses from Wilmslow and Manchester Airport. Some trains from Manchester, Wilmslow and Alderley Edge stop at Styal station
Getting there by car	Styal Country Park and Quarry Bank Mill are off the B5166 Wilmslow to Gatley road. The mill and country park are both signed from the A34 north of Wilmslow and also from Junction 6 of the M56. There is a large car park

The Tea Shops

Quarry Bank Mill (fee for car park unless NT members)
A DIY option is to have a picnic on the Mill meadow; supplies available from the Pantry in the mill yard. Open daily, (except Mondays, between October and mid-March). For a more substantial meal, there is the Mill Restaurant (licensed) off the mill yard. Children's menu available during school holidays.

Opening hours: summer, every day 10.30am to 5.00pm; winter, Tuesday to Friday 10.30am to 4.00pm; weekends, 10.30am to 4.30pm; Tel: 01625 527468.

Styal General Store & Tea Room

This avoids the car park entrance fee and keeps you away from the crowds. It's just a short distance away from the entrance to Quarry Bank Mill: drive past the entrance and take the first turn left into Styal village. Set behind what used to be the village post office, you'll find the tea room. There's plenty of outdoor seating and a good, basic range of home-made cakes, scones and other goodies for the hungry walker.

Opening hours: roughly, Easter to end of October, most days about 8am to 4pm, but essential to check in advance of visit. Tel: 01625 525 236.

Quarry Bank Mill

Now regarded as one of the finest working museums in the country, Quarry Bank Mill, Styal, was built by Samuel Gregg in the late eighteenth century with additions in early part of the nineteenth. It is typical of the early mills of the Industrial Revolution with its weaving sheds and warehouses.

Constructed in the Georgian style with a distinctive cupola, it sits alongside the River Bollin which provided the power that drove the spinning machines and looms. A special village with its own church, shop and school was built to house the workers. There was also an Apprentice House for the very young pauper children brought from London. The mill, surrounding woodlands, village and Apprentice House are now owned by the National Trust which has restored the mill, including the giant water wheel, to working order.

Opening hours: April to the end of September, Daily, 11.00am to 5.00 p.m; October to March, daily (except Monday) 11.00am to 4.00pm

Apprentice House with scarecrow

The Route

Regardless of which tea shop you plan to use, or where you have left your car, the walk starts from the car park for Quarry Bank Mill. Leave the car

Walk 24 Styal

park to the left of the entrance which, 10 metres beyond the payment kiosk, reaches the main approach drive to the mill. (This is forbidden to unauthorised traffic).

Turn right along this for a few metres but, by a large oak tree and a National Trust sign which reads, "Styal To The Woods", turn left onto an excellent maintained path which runs just to the left of a hedge.

Pass through two stiles until meeting a wider track by an information panel on the boundary of the North Woods. Turn right, this new path staying just inside the woodland boundary until it exits by two squeezer stiles in quick succession.

Stay forward to pass to the right of Norcliffe Chapel. According to the deeds of the trust establishing this place of worship it was built "for the worship of God and the furtherance of Christian Life free from the fetters of any written or unwritten declarations of faith". It is open every Sunday from Easter to the end of September between 2.30pm and 5.00pm.

Continue beyond the chapel and the subsequent lychgate to the remnants of the medieval cross which used to stand by the village green. After being damaged as the result of a road accident it was transferred to its present location and has since been skillfully restored.

By the cross turn left into the cobbled lane leading to an intersection in front of a row of redbrick cottages. There turn right so the cottages are on your left. By the last one keep the same line of direction between two hedges until meeting the road from Styal to Altrincham.

Cross to the facing wooden stile and footpath sign. Over the stile turn sharply to the left along the clearly defined path as it passes through a gateway some 50 metres to the right of a field corner. Once through that gateway turn sharply to the right to pass beneath some overhead wires to a stile. Maintain direction, still with a hedge on your right, to the B5166, the road from Wilmslow to Gatley.

Cross to the footpath sign opposite and follow your general line of direction by walking through the wide gap to the right of "Willow Cottage" to reach a stile after 20 metres which is quickly followed by a wooden kissing gate.

Cross the railway line by means of the footbridge to a second kissing gate which allows access to Styal golf course. Cross this by maintaining a straight line immediately to the right of a line of trees and shrubs and guided by a succession of waymarker poles until reaching a wooden seat by a small pond. Cross the surfaced road and stay to the right of a row of hawthorns for 50 metres to sign reading "Next Tee". Negotiate the stile to the right of this to exit from the golf course.

Stay to the right of a hedge for 40 metres before turning left over a wooden stile and then sharp right so maintaining the general line of direction to the left of a hedge.

On your left there is a large clump of dead trees rising out of a dried-up pond, the remnants of one of the many marl pits scattered over the Cheshire Plain. Marl was used extensively for spreading over land when it was ploughed, not to mention forming the basis of a good cricket pitch.

Negotiate a stile in the facing hedge by the field corner and then veer about 20 degrees to the left, aiming for an obvious stile in the hedge ahead.

Over that veer 45 degrees to the left, heading towards a stile in the next field corner. After this follow the well-defined path across a large open area of scrub consisting principally of scattered hawthorns, rosebay willowherb and tall grass.

At the first intersection of paths, after a distance of only 50 metres, continue forwards for a further 200 metres until meeting a second intersection. A few metres beyond this is a stile by an oak tree in a facing hedge. Ignore this stile. Instead, at the intersection, turn right to walk close to the hedge on your left. After 250 metres pass through a pair of old stone gateposts and, keeping "The Grange" on your left, advance until meeting Clay Lane.

Turn right. Initially this is surfaced and has bungalows on your left. However, beyond the final bungalow it reverts to a narrow, partially hedged lane.

Pass to the right of a metal gate carrying a "NO ENTRY" sign to reach an inverted Y-junction. Bear right to meet the Handforth to Styal road by Southfield Manor, now a nursing home. Turn right but, after 100 metres, go left over a wooden stile onto the path signed to Linney's Bridge. Stay to the left of the fence but, in the first field corner, make a right turn over a stile as the narrow path runs between wire fences.

Eventually it enters a small wood and winds its course between the trees to a Y-junction with a footpath finger post close to the road at Linney's Bridge.

Do not emerge onto the road. Turn right over a waymarked stile to follow a path signed to Quarry Bank Mill. Cross a small field, veering uphill and to the right to a wooden stile.

Continue to the left of a fence before curving left by a hawthorn tree and an elder to another stile. From this point continue along the boundary of the woods, following a line above a small wooded clough which is on your left.

In due course, the path swings left over a wooden footbridge to a waymarked stile. Beyond that, stay forward over a field while aiming for a stile located by the left-hand corner of a bungalow.

Proceed alongside this bungalow to a wooden footpath sign. Turn left over the railway footbridge and left again at the far side. Walk to the right of a hedge to another footpath sign. Turn right along the wide track by Wilmslow Albion Football Club's ground until emerging onto the B5166. Turn left along this for 10 metres and then go right into the approach road to Styal Country Park and Quarry Bank Mill.

Alternatively, if you prefer the tea room in Styal village (having first made sure that it will be open!), turn right, walk along the B5166 for about 300 metres and then take a left turn into Styal village. The Ship Inn is on your right and the tea room on your left.

Walk 25: Knutsford

Route	Knutsford - Tatton Mere - Old Hall - Tatton Hall - Melchett Mere - Tatton Mere - Knutsford
Start	The car park off King Street, Knutsford. Map reference SJ753786
Distance	6 miles
Map	OS Explorer 268, Wilmslow, Macclesfield & Congleton
Getting there by public transport	Knutsford is served by frequent daily (including Sunday) trains from Chester, Northwich, Altrincham, Stockport and Manchester Piccadilly. There are daily buses from Chester, Northwich, Altrincham, Warrington, Wilmslow (not Sunday) and Macclesfield (not Sunday)
Getting there by car	Knutsford is signed from Junction 19 of the M6 motorway. It is on the A50 between Warrington and Stoke-on-Trent. It may also be reached by the A5033 from Northwich, the A537 from Macclesfield and the B5085 from Wilmslow and Alderley Edge

The Tea Shop

If you arrive at the Courtyard Coffee House, King Street, Knutsford by Penny Farthing you are entitled to claim a free tea but, sadly, walkers have to pay. It would be true to say that this antique but romantic form of transport provides the theme for this most excellent of tea shops because inside there is a suspended display of about thirty of these two-wheeled machines. Another unusual attraction is the miniature American train which runs along the track fixed at the point where the walls and ceiling meet.

Even as you approach the setting is perfect. From King Street you pass through a passageway into a cobbled courtyard which probably existed when Mrs. Gaskell stayed in the town. The Courtyard Coffee House is the epitome of an ideal English tea room. Except at busy periods you can choose whether to sit in the light and airy conservatory or outside in the attractive courtyard .

The tea, of which several speciality brews are available, is served in large but elegant pots, matched by equally refined crockery. Unusually, too, there is a wide variety of coffees on offer. Amongst the soft drinks is Elderflower Champagne.

The menu matches the atmosphere with all dishes freshly prepared using seasonal ingredients wherever possible. Try the unusual soups or, for something more substantial, the Welsh Rarebit. At coffee or tea time, there is a tempting display of cakes and pastries, guaranteed to undo the calories expended on the walk.

Courtyard Coffee House

Opening hours: Mondays to Fridays, 10.00am to 4.30 p.m; Saturdays and Sundays, 10.00am to 5.00 p.m; Tel: 01565 653974.

Knutsford

Knutsford takes its name from King Canute who is reputed to have forded a stream there. As he removed his boots to empty the water out a wedding party came by. He wished the happy couple as many children as there were grains of sand falling out of his boots.

This legend has given rise to the custom of "Sanding the Streets" during the annual May Day celebrations. This involves creating designs and patterns by using coloured sands on the pavements.

Mentioned in the Domesday Book, Knutsford has a long and important history but it is best known as the setting for Mrs. Gaskell's novel, "Cranford", and this association between the town and author is perpetuated in monuments and street names. The Tourist Information Centre produces a very useful town guide for anyone wishing to stroll round after their visit to the Courtyard Coffee House.

Tatton

It is worth while to make several breaks in the course of this walk to visit the varied attractions of Tatton. Prehistoric remains have been excavated alongside Tatton Mere by archaeologists from Manchester University. Our route passes the Old Hall, precursor of the present Georgian mansion, home of the Egerton family. Both repay the time spent exploring their interiors. Children may also like to visit the Home Farm.

Full details of all the Tatton attractions along with opening times may be obtained by ringing the Tatton Infoline, (01625) 534435 or the main switchboard on (01625) 534400 or by writing to Administration, Tatton Park, Knutsford, Cheshire, WA16 6QN.

The Route

Take the lower exit from the car park and turn left for 25 metres before making a right turn onto the surfaced path which runs alongside the mere on Knutsford Moor.

This mere is noted as one of the largest areas of fen and reed swamp in Cheshire, containing examples of greater reed mace and tussock sedge. A large bird population embraces Canada geese, mute swans, tufted duck and ruddy duck.

Proceed beyond the mere and the pumping station, under the railway bridge and up to Mobberley Road. Turn left and walk along to the lay-by where you turn left again into Teal Avenue then Mallard Close which ends with a hump-back bridge over the railway line. The entrance to Dog Wood is immediately on your right. Dog Wood is noted locally for its population of wrens, blackbirds, blue tits, great tits and woodpeckers.

A wooden gate provides an entrance into Tatton Park and allows the path to continue alongside Tatton Mere until reaching a jetty. By this, turn right along a wide chatter track for 150 metres to a T-junction in front of a Scout camp site.

Turn left following the track through a large Z bend to pick-up a deer fence on your right as you traverse the open parkland. In late summer and early autumn look for the large flocks of lapwing roosting on the fields beyond this fence. Pass through a metal gate (this is often left open) to enter an impressive oak plantation, parts of which are used as a car park.

Maintain direction to a T-junction close by some toilets. Turn left down the slope for a distance of about 100 metres and, by the first junction, make a right turn along a surfaced track which is signed to the Old Hall, the Landscape History Trail and the Melchett Walk. (Booklets available from the Gift Shop include "Discover Tatton Park on Foot" and "Wartime Tatton".)

Stay to the right of another car park to pass to the left of the Old Hall. By the far corner of the boundary fence of the Old Hall and a display panel illustrating the story of "Tatton At War", make a sharp left turn onto a broad green path which traverses the parkland and makes for enjoyable walking.

Walk 25 Knutsford

To Altrincham

A5034

Airborne Memorial

N

Tatton Hall

Old Hall

P

Mere

A50

To Warrington

A50

Melchett Mere

T a t t o n

P a r k

Tatton Mere

A50

B5085

To Macclesfield

S

A5033

Knutsford

A50

To Holmes Chapel

A537

To Macclesfield

0   500m

After a considerable distance you will reach a T-junction by the very moving stone memorial to members of the parachute forces who trained at Tatton before heading off to the various theatres of war between 1940 and 1945.

Turn left and follow the clear path, staying to the right of a plantation until meeting the drive from the main entrance to Tatton Hall itself. Turn left towards Tatton Hall but, at the next junction, fork left along the drive signed to the Old Hall (if you wish to visit the Hall, turn right). You do not have to walk on the hard surface but may use the grass parkland on either side.

Eventually you will pass Melchett Mere on your right and, at the junction a short distance beyond, maintain direction towards the Knutsford entrance with Tatton Mere now a short distance away on your left.

At the entrance use the small gate to the right of the cattle grid and proceed through the impressive classical arch. 100 metres beyond, where the road bends to the right, stay forwards along the broad path to meet King Street. Turn left to pass the Courtyard Coffee Shop.

Opposite Mrs Gaskell's Tower, turn left into Cotton Shop Yard and, at the far end, emerge into the car park from which you started.

Walk 26: Dunham Massey

Route	Dunham Massey - Brickkiln Lane - Little Bollington - Bridgewater Canal - Dunham Town - Oldfield Lane - Dunham Forest Golf Course - Charcoal Lane - Dunham Massey
Start	The car park, Dunham Massey Park. Map reference SJ733875
Distance	4½ miles
Map	OS Explorer 268, Wilmslow, Macclesfield & Congleton; OS Explorer 276, Bolton, Wigan & Warrington
Getting there by public transport	Frequent daily (including Sunday) buses from Warrington and Altrincham pass the entrance to Dunham Massey Park
Getting there by car	Leave the M6 at junction 19 and take the A56 in the direction of Altrincham. At the Bowdon traffic lights turn left along the minor road signed to Partington. The entrance to Dunham Massey Park is a further half mile. From Manchester and Altrincham take the A56 Chester Road, turning right at the Bowdon traffic lights. There is a large car park (fee)

The Tea Shops

The Stables Restaurant is on the upper floor above the shop. It is a light, airy and spacious building of unusual length and with beamed ceiling and exposed brick walls. Unusually it has solid wooden tables and chairs to match.

The light lunches include a changing daily selection of hot dishes rolls with various fillings and soup with roll. There is a wonderful choice of home-made cakes including flapjacks, date and walnut, chocolate sponge, Victoria sponge and coffee sponge. An alternative is to have afternoon tea or scones with jam and cream. A speciality is Dunham Pudding served with cream or custard. A really fruity concoction, it certainly provides ample energy for the afternoon walker. There is a choice of coffees and a variety of speciality teas.

Opening hours: open daily 10.30 to 5pm (4pm in winter).

Alternatives

If you prefer not to pay the general admission charge to get your afternoon tea or morning coffee, there are alternatives just outside the park:

White Cottage Tea Room, Park Lane, Little Bollington, WA14 4TJ. A charming tea room run by Diane Harrison. Open Thursday 11am to 4pm and Friday to Sunday, 11am to 4pm. Home-made cakes and shortbread; sit inside or in the charming garden. Tel 0161 941 1695.

Lavender Barn Tea Room, Dog Farm, School Lane, Dunham Massey WA14 4TR. Set in a five-acre farm with lavender field. Wide range of teas and coffees, home-made cakes, light lunches. Open 10am to 4pm daily. Tel: 0161 941 4193.

Dunham Massey

This fine Georgian house was the home of the Earls of Stamford until 1976 when it passed into the ownership of the National Trust. It is renowned for its collections of furniture, family portraits and Huguenot silver. Currently extensive work is in hand to restore some of the fine avenues of trees to their original designs. An ancient Jacobean flour mill has been returned to working order. The parkland, which covers 250 acres, supports a fine herd of fallow deer and contains a slaughter house and an unusual deer barn.

The Route

Regardless of whether you have paid to get into the park, the start and finish points are the main car park – so you need to get there first! Having done that, leave the car park by the main entrance, turning left for some five metres along Charcoal Road. By the footpath sign to Bollington, turn left into Brickkiln Lane which is also signed to Bollington Mill.

Initially this wends its way through woodland with the brick boundary wall of Dunham park on your left but eventually it leaves the trees behind for open country with the River Bollin close by on the right.

By Bollington Mill, now converted into luxury apartments, turn right across the metal footbridge spanning the river and stay forward for a short distance along the very narrow road while passing the unusually named pub, "The Swan With Two Nicks"

The clock tower at Dunham Massey

Some 50 metres beyond, at a Y-junction, fork right along the cobbled lane signed as part of the Bollin Valley way, a medium distance linear route which follows the course of this Cheshire river from Macclesfield to the Manchester Ship Canal.

Pass under an arched canal bridge before turning immediately to the right to ascend a flight of five stone steps followed by a path onto the towpath of the Bridgewater Canal, where you turn left. Cross the Bollin Aqueduct followed by the bridge over Woodhouse Lane. Ten metres after passing beneath a redbrick, hump-backed bridge, turn left through a wooden kissing gate and left again up the slight slope to Back Lane.

Make another left turn for the short distance to the T-junction by St Mark's Church and opposite the former Post Office (now closed) in Dunham Town. Go right into School Lane but, after a mere ten metres and by a footpath sign, turn left into another lane signed to Oldfield Lane.

Pass to the left of a white cottage, following the lane as it runs to the right of the churchyard to a wooden stile. Over this it is flanked by

Walk 26 Dunham Massey

hedgerows until reaching a three-arrowed footpath post. Turn right across a field, passing to the right of a solitary tree to a stile with a footpath sign alongside which provides access to Oldfield Lane.

Turn right but, after 20 metres and by another sign, make a left turn. Cross another field to a sign with three arrows. Turn left along the path signed to Altrincham, staying close to the hedge on your left until the first stile provides an entry onto Dunham Forest Golf Course.

Taking your direction from the arm of the footpath finger post, veer slightly to the right across the links until meeting a broad track by tee number 7. Turn left along the track for a short distance until reaching a small toilet block on your right. Some 80 metres further on, turn acute right by tee number 12, across the fairway to a gap in the hedgeonto a narrow path. Continue until you reach Charcoal Lane.

Cross diagonally right to a very conspicuous and large white gate with an extremely tall ladder stile alongside. Over this it is possible to follow the surfaced driveway for approximately one mile if you wish to head directly back to Dunham Hall. However, a more interesting alternative is to fork left almost immediately beyond the stile, taking the well-worn grass path and staying with it until it forms a T-junction with a similar path flanked by an avenue of tall trees. Turn right along this to walk by the deer paddocks on your way back to the Hall and the Stables Restaurant.

After refreshments turn left and left again under the archway to cross the moat before turning right for the short distance to the car park, or wherever your car is parked.

Walk 27: Lymm

Route	Lymm Library - Lymm Dam - The Avenue - Booth's Lane - Mersey Brook Lane - Bridgewater Canal - Lymm Library
Start	The car park by Lymm Library. Map reference SJ681874
Distance	3½ miles
Map	OS Explorer 276, Bolton, Wigan & Warrington
Getting there by public transport	Lymm is served by frequent daily (including Sundays) buses from Warrington and Altrincham
Getting there by car	Lymm is on the A56 which runs from Junction 7 of the M56 Motorway to Warrington. It is also signed from the M6 at Junction 20. The library car park is signed from the A56

The Tea Shops

Our first recommendation is Sexton's Bakery and Café at 2, Eagle Brow in the centre of Lymm village. The modern wooden tables and chairs are spread discreetly around the shop and the seating is further supplemented by a small bar with tall stools. There is a fine Welsh dresser with a display of preserves and pickles.

You may select from a freshly buttered croissant to any of the pies, cakes and scones displayed in the bakery section, all accompanied by cups of freshly ground coffee or speciality tea or soft drink. For more substantial fare, there is a choice of soups, jacjet potatoes and casseroles.

Opening hours: Monday to Saturday, all year, 8.30 am to 4.30 pm. Tel: 01925 75369

An alternative is The Terrace Brasserie at 11, The Cross, just a short distance from Sexton's, towards the ancient Lymm Cross. A great range of breakfasts (served 8.30 am to noon) ranging from traditional to veggie, with more unusual offerings of French toast with bacon & maple syrup, Eggs Benedict or smoked salmon and poached eggs on a toasted muffin. Wide range of salads, platters and hot dishes.

Opening hours: 8.30 to 4pm, Tuesday to Saturday. Tel: 01925 751421

Lymm

Lymm is an attractive village clustered around its ancient market cross and stocks and nestling beneath the parish church with its pinnacled tower. Once a centre of fustian manufacture, it is dominated by the Bridgewater Canal, now used by pleasure boats but initially the main commercial artery of the Industrial Revolution in the North West of England.

One of Lymm's attractions is the Dingle, a gorge 100 feet deep overhung with foliage and approached from the centre of the village.

The Route

Descend through the car park towards the canal. By the Boat Stage veer right down the cobbles to Bridgewater Street. Turn right but, at the far end turn left into Eagle Brow. Within a few metres, and immediately before the road bridge, turn right into the Dingle, passing a footpath sign after about 50 metres.

Continue along the path through this wooded glen, its steeply sloping sides festooned with ivy, staying to the right of the green railings and Bradley Brook. Where the railings corner away to the left notice the waterfall under the arch of the road bridge. Climb the steps to reach the A56. Cross directly to the footpath sign and take the path alongside Lymm Dam which is on your left.

Attempts to landscape it on a grand design by Lord Leverhulme were abandoned but there are still relics of the aborted enterprise along our route. By the first corner of the dam, turn right onto a signed footpath which runs along the west bank through a mixture of deciduous trees. Beyond a wooden bench, while the reservoir curves away to the left, the path pursues its onward course but the two meet again shortly before a wooden barrier with a notice board and footpath sign adjacent.

Through the barrier an intersection is reached. Look to the left to see the ornamental bridge, part of the Leverhulme grand design. However, make a right turn at this intersection to reach a road after ten metres. Turn left along The Avenue which, in the French fashion, is lined on both sides with Lombardy poplars so, in the middle of Cheshire, creating a continental landscape.

At the far end of The Avenue turn right along the B5158, using the grass verge and then the pavement and passing Turner's Pool on your left. 100 metres beyond the 30 mph signs make a left turn into Booth's Lane. After some 200 metres, and beyond the last house, turn right by the footpath sign to follow a path which runs between a wire fence on the left and a series of garden fences on the right.

Ahead is a wide-ranging view of the Mersey Valley and beyond into South Lancashire with Thelwall Viaduct conspicuous closer to hand. How pleasant it is to be travelling at a snail's pace on foot rather than hurtling along the M6 Motorway in a tin box at 70 mph. This advantage certainly allows time for spotting the small tortoiseshell butterflies and the many pheasants hereabouts.

On reaching a T-junction with a three-armed footpath post make a left turn to walk between two barbed wire fences. After a wooden squeezer stile keep to the boundary of a large field with a hedge on the left. 50 metres before reaching a conspicuous way-marked stile, and by a footpath sign, turn right over a wooden footbridge and stile to walk immediately to the left of a hedge until a further stile permits entry onto Massey Brook Lane with the Bridgewater Canal facing you.

Turn right along Massey Brook Lane, keeping to the pavement until the junction with the A56. Turn left along Camsley Lane, as the A56 is known at this point, and cross the concrete bridge spanning the Bridgewater Canal. At the far end turn right down the cobbled Yeald Brow and then maintain direction along the canal towpath. Enterprising house-holders on both sides of the water have utilised the canalside for hen runs, lawns and small strips of flower or vegetable gardens.

Lymm Cross

After approximately one mile the canal passes beneath Brookfield Bridge. Continue further along the towpath until reaching the hump-backed Lymm Bridge. Immediately before this turn left through a small metal gate and proceed in front of a row of cottages to New Road.

Turn right, re-crossing the canal to enter The Cross. Descend the hill to pass the actual cross on your left before swinging right over another bridge to enter Eagle Brow. After 10 metres, and by Barclay's Bank, turn right into Bridgewater Street for a few metres before veering left by the Post Office to climb to the canal and the boat stage. There, turn left for the final few metres to your starting point.

Walk 28: Wilmslow

Route	Moor Lane - Lindow Moss - Saltersley - Morley Green - Newgate - Moor Lane
Start	Ned Yates Garden Centre, Moor Lane, Wilmslow. Map reference SJ823802
Distance	3 miles
Map	OS Explorer 268, Wilmslow, Macclesfield & Congleton
Getting there by public transport	Regular buses to Wilmslow town centre
Getting there by car	From the town centre, drive along Water Lane and turn left after traffic lights, down Hawthorn Street. Turn right at the Carter's Arms along Chapel Lane, which becomes Moor Lane. At the end of Moor Lane, keep right and you soon come to the garden centre - there is a sign to direct you. Most times you can park in the garden centre car park while you complete your walk (please ask first); if not, park considerately on the road

The Tea Shop

Ned Yates Garden Centre is tucked away in the south-west corner of Wilmslow, at the end of Moor Lane. The light and modern Seedhouse Restaurant is behind the shop and open-air seating is available in the summertime. At breakfast time, choices include croissants, omelettes and a vegetarian breakfast; with morning coffee or afternoon tea there's a scrumptious array of cakes and, for lunch, tempting "lite bites" (soups, bagels, savoury tarts) and, to satisfy the hungriest of walkers, a range of pies and speciality platters.

Opening hours: summertime, Monday to Saturday, 9.30 to 4.30pm, Sunday 10.00 to 4.30pm; closes half an hour earlier in winter. Tel: 01625 522128.

The Route

Continue beyond the garden centre in the same direction as you arrived, passing Moor Lane House on your right. Follow the tarmac lane as it bears

Walk 28 Wilmslow

N

Rossmere

Newgate Farm

Newgate

To Wilmslow

Lindow Moss

Barlow Farm

Wilmslow

0   250m

right. After a few minutes, the lane bears left into Lindow Court Park, but you go straight ahead. To be absolutely pedantic, the right of way goes to the left of the hedge, but most walkers just keep to the left of the large white gate and continue straight ahead on tarmac for about 20m before bearing diagonally right to a concrete bridge. You are now in the bizarre landscape of Lindow Moss where, although the peat workings are unattractive, they provide a habitat for many species and both silver birch and heather flourish on the acidic soil.

Continue straight ahead, crossing footbridges as necessary. Ignore turns to the left or right until a more substantial bridge heads off to the left (yellow waymark). Cross this to an area thick with bracken and pass a small private nature reserve on your left. Go through an avenue of silver birch and you reach a track which serves Saltersley Hall – an ancient building that was, in the 19th century, a staging post for packhorse trains carrying salt from Northwich to Yorkshire. In the 1980s you could have bought afternoon tea from an elderly Mrs Croxall; many such farmhouses used to offer refreshments to weary walkers, prior to draconian EU health regulations.

Turn right along the track and, after 80m, turn left at the end of a holly hedge. Cross the waymarked stile and continue with the hedge on your left to another footpath sign. Turn right here and you will soon see a large fishing lake, formed as the result of sand extraction; in the course of this the original footpath was flooded and a long battle ensued to establish the pleasant path along which you are now walking. Follow the waymarked path, keeping the lake on your right, to a little beyond the extreme end of the lake. Cross a stile and turn left along the track, passing bungalows to both left and right.

At a cross-roads, turn left along a lane signed as 'Bridle Path to Morley'. Follow this lane, which soon becomes a wide track. Just where this track bears right at a gate, and a narrower one continues straight ahead, turn right along a track with a yellow waymark. Continue to a junction of wide, stony tracks and bear left at a waymark to enter the landscaped former landfill site known to locals as Newgate Tip. The landscaping is a credit to the authorities.

At the highest point of this track, turn right (waymark) on a wide grassy track and enjoy the fabulous views all around you. I saw rabbits on the ground and buzzards high above me last time I was here – quite a place! The metal flues you can see are to burn off excess methane from the decaying waste. This avoids having the whole lot blow up, which might detract from the enjoyment of your imminent afternoon tea.

Descend to a junction of paths and go straight ahead, following the line of a wooden fence to a steel gate, opening onto Newgate. Turn left and, after 100m, turn right at Springfield House (footpath sign) along a track. You are now back in the Lindow Moss area, though not with peat extraction. There are many paths to follow – and to get lost on – so follow these directions carefully: at the first intersection you reach, turn right along a wider track, passing some (currently) ramshackle stables. Continue for 300m or so, passing a house on the right. Ignore the first track on your left – instead, bear right and continue for another 150m to a clear T-junction; this is where you turn left. It's easy from here: continue all the way along this track, passing alongside a gate, to a tarmac road; at a more major road (Moor Lane), turn right and you're almost back to your car – and the prospect of morning coffee or afternoon tea should spur you on.

Seedhouse Restaurant at Ned Yates Garden Centre

Also from Sigma Leisure:

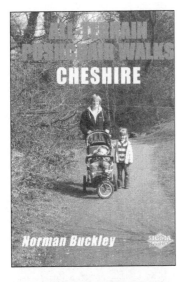

All-Terrain Pushchair Walks
Cheshire
Norman Buckley
30 graded walks, from level routes around pretty Cheshire villages to more adventurous hikes across the hillsides. Detailed directions and a map are provided for each route, together with some stunning photographs.
£7.95

Best Pub Walks in Cheshire
2nd Edition
Jen Darling
This is the second edition of a guidebook to the walks and pubs of Cheshire.
"I was delighted to be asked to put a few words on paper ... this book brings together a series of suggestions for your enjoyment."
– John Ellis, Cheshire Tourism
£8.99

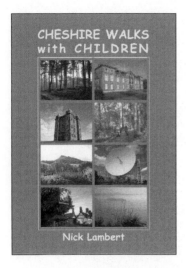

Cheshire Walks With Children 2nd Edition
Nick Lambert

Now completely revised and updated, this was the first in our "walks with children" series and has quickly become a firm favourite. There are 30 walks, ranging in length, together with things to look out for and questions to answer along the way make it an entertaining book for young and old alike.

£8.99

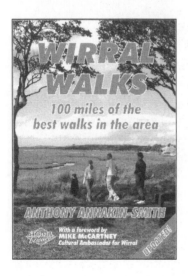

Wirral Walks 2nd Edition
100 miles of the best walks in the area
Anthony Annakin-Smith

A completely revised and updated edition of this popular collection of 25 walks from around 2 to 10 miles, covering a total of 100 miles through the best of the local landscape. The author's careful research highlights the interesting and unusual features seen along each route.

£8.99

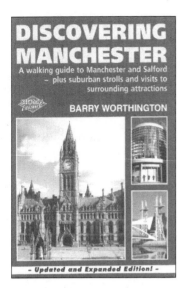

Discovering Manchester
2nd Edition
Barry Worthington

This stylish walking guide doubles as a detailed account of the city's architecture, its history and tourism attractions. There are walks throughout Manchester including such major entertainment and cultural centres as the Bridgewater Hall, Urbis, the Museum of Science and Industry, the Lowry and many more. Explore the entire city – from the Corn Exchange to G-Mex, from the Cathedral to Affleck's Palace.
£10.99

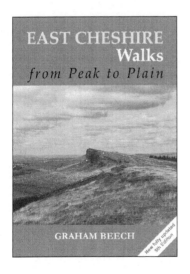

East Cheshire Walks
from Peak to Plain
Graham Beech

East Cheshire is a land of contracts — from rugged hills to gently rolling countryside. Thanks to this variety, there really is something for walkers of all interests and abilities — and *East Cheshire Walks* is by far the most comprehensive guidebook to the area, with almost 40 walks ranging from 3 to 20 miles covering a total of over 250 miles. There are easy ambles in Cheshire's mid-county pasture land, interesting strolls alongside rivers and canals, and a selection of more strenuous hikes in the foothills of the Peak District.
£8.99

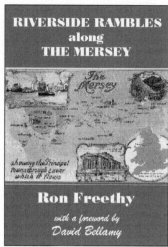

Riverside Rambles along The Mersey
Ron Freethy
with a foreword by David Bellamy

This is far more than a guidebook for walkers, it is also a portrait of one of the world's greatest rivers – once so polluted that Michael Heseltine described the state of the Mersey basin as "an affront to civilised society". Nowadays, however, salmon pass through the estuary, wildlife abounds along the entire catchment area and a rich and diverse coastline attracts a huge variety of birdlife.

Featuring 30 walks short, gentle walks (mostly circular). Explore the unique scenery, ecology and heritage of this area.
£8.99

Best Pub Walks in the Dark Peak &
Best Pub Walks in the White Peak
Les Lumsdon and Martin Smith

These two books, both by Les Lumsdon and Martin Smith, provide comprehensive coverage of the entire Peak District. Inspiring walks and welcoming pubs enable walkers to appreciate the history, landscape and personalities of the area. These books were published by us originally in the 1980s and have recently been completely updated to ensure accuracy. Each book costs ***£8.99***

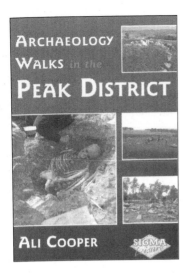

Archaeology Walks in The Peak District
Ali Cooper

These walks explore archaeological sites where there are visible pre-historic features in the landscape: Bronze age barrows, stone circles, caves, mines and much more. Walks are from 3 to 12 miles and are fully illustrated. The book includes an introduction to the study of archaeology and a glossary of the terminology used. Brief descriptions of the major finds on the walks are included, plus a bibliography for those who wish to delve deeper. Ali Cooper has an MA in archaeology and is a keen outdoors enthusiast.

£8.99

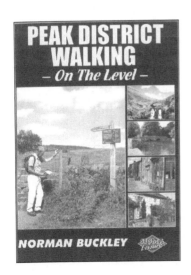

Peak District Walking – On The Level
Norman Buckley

Some folk prefer easy walks, and sometimes there's just not time for an all-day yomp. In either case, this is definitely a book to keep on your bookshelf. Norman Buckley has had considerable success with "On The Level" books for the Lake District and the Yorkshire Dales.

The walks are ideal for family outings and the precise instructions ensure that there's little chance of losing your way. Well-produced maps encourage everybody to try out the walks - all of which are well scattered across the Peak District.

£8,99

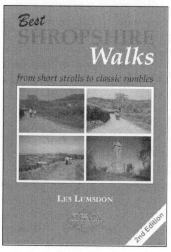